The Departure Of Solitude

The Departure Of Solitude

Tony Webb

Matador
9 Priory Business Park
Kibworth Beauchamp
Leicestershire LE8 0RX, UK
Tel: (+44) 116 279 2299
Fax: (+44) 116 279 2277
Email: books@troubador.co.uk
Web: www.troubador.co.uk/matador

ISBN 978-1783064-816

British Library Cataloguing in Publication Data.
A catalogue record for this book is available from the British Library.

Typeset in Aldine by Troubador Publishing Ltd

Matador is an imprint of Troubador Publishing Ltd

In memory
Of my father
David Charles Webb
Who also had a few good stories
Of his own to tell
And who gave me my smile
Miss you and Thank you

Contents

Preface

So you've picked up this book and you're wondering, what's this all about? Where's he heading if the title is anything to go by? To a far flung place in the sun, or some other-worldly adventure maybe? But within these pages you'll find hope, love, sadness, happiness and memories that maybe you can relate to at some point in your life. I've asked myself many times, "Why write a book , what's the purpose for it and what do I hope to achieve?"

Even now I don't know the right answer to these questions, all I can say is I wrote my first story at the age of twelve (around ten stories at that age).

I didn't write again 'til I was twenty three, again ten stories or so, written this time at a low point in my life.

Fast forward some ten years later and there I am again in a place alone and despairing, nothing but a mobile phone at hand. So I began to type some words, then more, and then yet more. I found it almost impossible to stop. Addictive maybe? Yes, I have to agree with that term indeed.

Posting the first short story to a networking site, I was given feed back that spurred me on.

The stories here, created in a dark room with very little light, sound or warmth, are from my own mind, some from my past experiences. Others were written about and for friends, loved ones that are here with me or that have passed on from our lives. A few created from daydreams I've had at any given time.

What you take away from this book and how you feel when you finish it are your emotions and yours alone. Not unless you choose to share how you feel with another, as it is always wonderful to share.

And remember, no matter what life throws at you, there's always a story to be had and a lesson to be learned from it. As my father used to say to me;

"Son, life's not a bowl of cherries, not each day is as sweet as the next."

Indeed my dad was right.

You see Dad,

I didn't forget that, not now, not ever.

My Departure of Solitude

When the music played I was
In the dark,
I longed for that loneliness
And the surrender of my own heart
I sat there writing
On the bare naked ground,
Wanting my isolation to be
Lost and found
With the doors locked and no
Exits I can see,
I talked to the voices that continued
To plague me
The pain of the stillness was
My only friend,
And not the ink that flowed from that
Blood soaked pen
These things that I write are a
Part of my mind,
You just think they're words to pass
The time
But what you don't know and what
You fail to see,
That within this book lie
Parts of me
I give you a glimpse at what you
Might call madness,
But for many others it's a lifetime

1

Of misery and sadness
But that was long ago in a place
Far from this,
I unlocked the room and left that
Cold dark abyss
Please read these verses and some
Call them stories,
They are chapters of my life of
Hope ,love and glory
So read on with this book whether it's
Second hand or bought
Brand new,
For this was my struggle my
Departure of solitude.

Skylar

Sitting there in the morning sun, he plays with his toys as the
beams of daylight slip past the trees outside and into his
bedroom, warming the floor he sits on.

Picking up each toy brick he studies each groove to the utmost
detail, life's little mysteries that we fail to see or be enchanted
by as we grow, losing that childlike magic within us all.

The snap of each one as they click together is all that can be heard
from his room, as he builds each masterpiece brick by brick.

"Good morning son, how did you sleep?" His father says as he sits
down and descends to his tiny world. With his legs crossed he
strokes the back of his sons head.

"So what you building today?" his dad asks

His son holds up an unfinished creation

"Ah, monsters again I see, but every time a different one. You're so
clever son; I hope one day you will tell me how you do it."

A smile graces the child's face and then he returns to his amazing
world of bricks and silence.

For the child holds his words deep within himself, but his
expressions and skill at his fingertips speak volumes. Until that
is, the age of four, when his inner voice finds a way to leave his
lips and he starts to talk.

He's sensitive and quiet but smart, bright just like the beams of
sunlight that shone in his room as a young boy. He loves
dinosaurs and can name each one off by heart. He also likes
the world of computers.

"Son, remember whatever you want in life is possible."

"Is it Dad? Do I dare to dream and want to be like others, or
dream that they were all like me?"

"Son, you can only be who you are and I wouldn't change that one bit. You are my son, a part of me and I love you all the same."

He hugs his son as he goes off to school. But there are those that don't understand him, and they don't want to. They look at him in an odd way and react in ways that are hurtful. For kids can be kind and brilliant, but also cruel. Picking on him because he sees things differently and it's strange to them. The name calling, tripping him over in the school hallways, the abuse goes on as he remains silent in his suffering. Even when his wrists get broken by a tormentor, still he remains silent. He stays on his own, a loner doing the things that make him happy. He's a young boy with a huge heart, always willing to help others, wanting to let those in, but instead keeps them at a distance.

The phone rings and his dad asks "Son, how about we go to the zoo and see what fun can be had?" And there's that smile again.

"Great Dad! Can't wait to see you, I wish you lived closer, be so cool if you did!"

And his dad fights back the tears over the phone as he holds it so tight with his knuckles glowing white.

"I'll see you soon son, it's a long drive but Dad won't let you down."

As he says goodbye and the phone goes silent, his father's back is pressed against wall as he slides down it, hands draped over his knees as pearls of tears carve their way down his face. They fall and are lost, soaked into his clothes. He takes a twelve hour drive across the state to see his son. The door opens and his son rushes out to meet him.

"Dad it's so good to see you!"

His dad scruffs up his hair and cuddles him.

"Son whether it's twelve hours or twelve days, I'd travel whatever distance to reach you."

"I know you would Dad, I know you would."

They head to the zoo and it's a wonderful day as they feed the animals and get up close to the giraffes.

"Dad why do others treat me differently?" his son asks.

And his dad stretches out his hand and strokes the giraffe and replies

"Skylar son, the doctors said you were different and people are afraid of what they don't understand."

His son says "How so?"

And his dad replies "Things aren't always black and white or even right and wrong. It's reading between the lines and many fail to see that, they miss the beauty with all its mysteries. It eludes them and they want to lash out."

His son Skylar tilts his head to one side and says

"Dad, you always have a way with words and expressing them to me."

As they walk away and he puts his arms around his son's shoulders and whispers to him "You are different, you can read and see between the lines while others can't. And for all the doctors said and did for you, remember most importantly; you are unique, you are my son!"

For Aric W. Hoogerwerf
For your son Skylar

Being different is amazing
Whether you have
A learning disability or not ,
You are a bright dazzling boy
And I hope the world
Stops, listens and sees you.

Worlds Apart

A little girl asks her father "What do you think I can be when I'm older Daddy?"

The father picks her up and carries her around on his back. "You can be anything you want to be my love; there are no rules to say you can't be anything your dream's desire. So if you wish to see the stars closer than most, then I will help you to ascend into the blue yonder, and smile because I know the stars will dazzle brighter because you are with them."

She cuddles her father and holds on as they spin in circles like we all have at that tender age. Now the little girl sits looking up at the big blue sky and thinks "So pretty yet so far away."

As the sun twinkles through the trees and makes her face glitter in the beams of the day, a little bird lands next to her, bobbing its head side to side and looking at her, it starts to chirp. The little girl reaches out to touch it and it flies away into the distance. Rather than being sad, the girl's face lights up and she runs into the house.

"Daddy, Daddy a small bird flew down and sat with me, it was so close, closer than the stars, I could have touched it!"

The father says "Ahhh you have found your calling then, the call of the Natural World."

"Oh yes Daddy I have, and to be with them is my dream."

The father strokes her hair and says "Then go get your dream and I will help you as much as I can."

As the hands of time rotate, it sees the little girl grow into a young woman in a blink of her father's eyes. She still loves the wild, but like leaves that float downstream, they have both drifted apart. He tires of her dream and wants her to forget about it as he feels it's a waste of her life.

"Dad you said I could do anything I dreamt of, and this is who I am now, I'm still that little girl but somehow, you've become distant, like that bird that flew away."

He says "Your time is wasted on such worthless dreams, where's the riches and glory in what you do?"

She cries but a fury leaves her lungs. "Worthless you say? How would you know? The riches you talk of are rewards. Nursing an animal back to health! And this glory will take me further than the stars! Whatever happened to helping me?"

He turns and walks out of the room and this leaves her thinking, will it ever be like it was before?

But if he's not careful she will walk out into the wide world, and he will lose that little girl he cherished only yesterday.

So if your child has a dream, whether it's reaching for the stars or building a city under the sea,

Don't drift away from them

Dream with them and help them see that the sky isn't the limit

Anything is possible if you dare to dream.

For Carley Jackson
I hope you and your father drift closer together
And that you both reach your stars as one.

The Promise

I sat with many friends one evening long ago. We talked of our
hopes, dreams and fears. What we'd all like to do, to be and
where we would end up. We all had our own far fetched
dreams that seemed impossible to reach. But we were young
and felt invincible.

"What are your dreams?" I asked my company of companions as I
lifted a bottle of beer to my lips. They all gave great replies.

"Tone I want to be rich and have a fast and hot car." said my
friends with eagerness

I replied "I'll take the riches part, but to be honest I'd give most of
it away, one man only needs so much. And forget the car, I'll
walk everywhere."

My five friends all spoke of women, flashy watches and great
fame'n'fortune.

"I hope you guys get your dreams but if one or more of us should
need help, promise we'll be there for each other no matter
what."

We all raised our drinks and we cheered.

"Hang on a minute, Tone," said my good friend "You didn't say
what dreams you are chasing?"

I had hoped to avoid telling my wishes, but it was only fair that I
told them, just like they had told me theirs. I sat looking at my
bottle of beer and slowly peeling the label off, trying not
to tear it.

"I am unsure to be honest. Maybe travel and see the world, write a
story about us all and maybe stumble across love."

The laughter could be heard throughout the bar and people

looked and shook their heads at the noise we made. But we cared not…

"Love, now there's a dream that'll drive you mad." said my friend who sat next to me. I put my arm around him and told him "David, love may take me to the far edges of the world and I may have many adventures and jot them down in a scrap book. Wherever I am, you'll all be with me."

I watched as he knocked back a beer with a love for it that was slightly uneasy to see. We spoke for hours and talked of memories that made our hearts ache.

I said "Guys, years from now we'll look back at these days and have many reunions just like this."

They sat and laughed; hell, they even threw crisps at me and called me a soppy sod. But we did agree that we would do so. How amazing we felt sitting there, all six of us together. Friendships that I hoped would stand the test of time.

We drank all we could and sang all night. What a sight to behold and our god-awful voices that make me smile now. As I recall, we finished our drinks and stepped out into the coolness of the night. We shook hands and hugged one another and each headed home, our own paths to take.

Time passed, and we lost touch. I wish I could tell you that we kept good to our word, but sadly time shows no mercy. For all my friends had passed on from this life. They found their dreams but with them came many nightmares that go hand in hand, for fast cars and faster women had burned them out before their time, all apart from one, 'David.'

Who was now lost to the demon drink and too far out of reach. I saw him the other day; he passed by but didn't even recognise me. I stopped him and said "My dear friend David, it's me, it's Tone."

He stared straight through me, like a shop window that had closed down.

"Who are you, get the fuck away from me, get out my way, I don't know you and couldn't care less about you."

I reached out to put my hand on his shoulder, "It's me, Tony, come on you must remember?"

He pushed me away and staggered with a bag that now held his five new friends waiting to be opened and drunk.

I can't explain how I felt right there and then. Standing across the road from the bar where we all dreamed some years before.

I sit and think of our dreams, now just a painful memory and a lost, past time. I wish so much to turn back the clock and steer my friends onto clearer paths. But they're gone now and I'm all that remains.

I did travel some, and can recall many adventures I have had and people I've met. I did jot down some of my moments that touched and changed my life and hope that I did my friends proud, who now look on from a place too distant for my eyes to view.

But as for finding love?

I had it once, but like a candle that melts down to the last wilting flicker it went out. I guess I am lucky to have had it, if only for a fleeting moment. I hope to find it again one day. All I long for now is that broken promise I wish we had all kept. That me and my friends would be there for each other no matter what.

As I sit here writing this now, the tears carving their way down my shabby face, I know there is hope at finding love. But to find such amazing friends again is a dream I continue to dream.

Old Flames

I loved a woman a lifetime ago,
She was more dazzling than
The jewels in the snow
She stole my heart and spoke of love,
Her eyes were more amazing
Than the stars above
The days were short and the nights
So tender,
I'd cross a desert, fight an army for you,
I would not surrender
That was long ago and my mind
Still strays,
Across ocean tides to steal your gaze
How I long for her touch and her
Gentle kiss,
It's been many years, but it's you
That I miss
I have not the power to turn
Back time,
I know you still love me until
The end of time
Life is too short to not take a chance,
Love is a melody, take my hand
Let us dance
My mind is set and my heart is free,
Walk with me now and let
Our hearts be,
For this is life and when will it end?
Say you'll stay and we'll be
More than friends.

Sis

What's the unspoken connection between two sisters?
Is it starting and finishing each other's sentences?
Knowing that when one is sad, the other feels that pain too?
Or maybe that instant when one of them knows when the phone
    will ring?
There were two sisters, so very close; closer than a reflection in a
    mirror. As they grew so did their bond.
"When I grow old, will you take care of me and still love me when
    I have not the strength to speak?"
"I will my love" she said to her.
"But what if I should fade? Will you remember me for all time
    and light a candle for me on my birthday?"
Her sister kissed her hand.
"I will, and everyday I will sing a song to remember you by."
The two sisters continued their lives as we all do, with wonder
    and amazement. Growing up and seeing life's little puzzles,
    making them ask all the right questions, but times change and
    the sisters move to different paths. One sister lives life to the
    fullest, seeking fun and amusement.
The other falls in love and her sense's become dulled. That free
    spirit that she once had is burnt out by a lover who wants to
    own her like a jail maker guarding his stock.
Again time drifts on, and the two sisters drift almost out of sight,
    like a boat sinking to the dark abyss of the ocean.
But the sister still feels a connection, a sense that her world is
    wilting and knows that somewhere her sister is hurting.
She finds her sister again and helps her break free from the ball
    and chain that has kept her prisoner for so long.

"I knew you'd come, I felt it; that long lost feeling that we had.
     When we were little girls I asked for you to come."
"I know you did."
The sisters embrace each other like wind and time.
"I said I will always love you, no matter how much you hurt me."
They leave that cell of emptiness for the last time. Now they sit
     and remember old times of when they were young, recalling
     their childhood dreams.
"Do you remember what you said you'd do if I should fade?"
"I do, I said I would sing a song everyday to remember you by and
     light a candle on your birthday."
She smiles at her sister as her face settles like rain on a thorny
     rose. "My dear sister, today you sing your first song. For today
     I start a journey that has one bittersweet end."
Then it dawns on her, but she knew deep down in her heart what
     was to come to pass. Days skip by, nights play out in a silence
     so loud it's deafening. Now in a warm bed she looks and sees
     her sister sleeping in a chair next to the bed.
She whisper's "Sis, I have to go now. I am sorry I am always
     leaving you, but please forgive me for I am tired and have to
     fade."
She close's her eyes and the room saddens in a blanket of
     bittersweet bliss.
As the sister wakes, she sees that she has gone; she's there, but
     removed from pain and at peace.
"I didn't need to say goodbye, as I knew you were going; but we
     both knew that, didn't we?"
Sisters are more than just friends,
They are far more than the moon
That sways the ocean tides
And that's because sisters' love for each other is
Far more gracious
Than anything I can express.

Cai

I had an amazing friendship once. Have you ever had that? An intense bond that's so overwhelming and personal, that when it's gone it shatters your world and all you long for is the hands of time to stop and go back.

I sat long ago in a quiet corner; I was given up and left to chance. Watching as people passed by not even spending a moment to look at me. I watched as others were touched and loved instantly. But not for me as I lay my head down and my eyes say it all. No hope for me; I wander, abandoned and unwanted as that's what happens to so many of us, but chance deals many hands in life and I was dealt an amazing one.

I lay there and hear soft footsteps, but not so soft that I can't hear them. My eyes open and looking down on me is a set of eyes and a tender smile.

"Wow!" I thought "This amazing woman wants me!"

And she bends down and strokes my chin "You're beautiful," she says "Please come with me."

I bound forward and we crash to the floor together. She kisses my face and I look on, saying in my heart "Take me home."

She does, to meet and become part of a new family. No words are spoken between us; for a friendship and love like ours, words are not needed. She tells me secrets and I keep them, for our trust for one another is deep and strong. We play fight and she pins me down but I let her win and she doesn't know that.

"You and me Cai, always" she says, as that's my name.

"Always you and I. There will never be another like you."

And she cuddles me 'til I fall asleep.

We chase each other in the park, playing hide and seek with
Michael and Chloe.

"Hey you, you will give me away. Get down and hide."

But I just stand there and give the game away like the big softie I
am. She wrestles me to the floor, puts her head next to mine
and whispers "You're such a big part of my life Cai, I love you,
I always will," as she nestles up against me, "If I lost you I
couldn't go on."

I stand and nod towards Michael and Chloe who are having a
picnic. "They will be there for you." I think to myself.

For there will be another, and many more need such loving
homes, and we run off together playing catch and being free.

The nights are quiet as I lay at her side on the bed, we curl up and
she falls asleep.

"You have given me so much in just a short space of time and I
have said very little, but you know I am grateful for my life
and my family."

Seven years pass so quickly. Too quick. The day dawns and
Catherine finds me lying down and weak. "What's up Cai?
Come on, up you get."

But I am a dead weight, I can't move and I only just raise my head.

"Come boy, come on get up, Cai please, please get up boy." and
her hands tremble to her lips as she lays my head on her lap.
"Come on boy you are going to be ok."

I feel tears fall like a fresh shower of rain in winter but I can't
move, I lay there, my eyes blinking as my breathing slows.

She says "I will carry you; bear your weight in my arms to find
help."

She does, but unknown to her, it's too late. I hold on for those last
tender moments, and as she slips from the room with just a
little hope that I will make it, I sigh and let out a gentle bark
one last time, as I slip from this life to the next and leave my
loving family. As I go to play hide and seek with so many
others like me.

For Catherine Wooler
In memory of Cai.
Who passed away 6/9/2010
When we lose those that are close to us
It seems that the pain will never ease
And the same can be said for the love of our animals
For they become part of us and our family
And those who choose not to have such friendships and bonds
Are missing out on a special magic that never fades
For you Cai
May you run the parks of the skies
Until Catherine calls your name again.

The Gift

A wise man came across many men one day long ago. They were
masters of steel and brought on others' pain and death. As he
tried to pass them he was stopped by the master of them all.

"Ha! Look at this old man. What do you want old man? A new
body by the looks of it…"

The old man stands motionless, "Tell me great lord what is your
gift? For everybody has a gift."

He replies, "Indeed I do, I have a great gift, I am legendary with a
blade."

The frail man shakes his head, "How is that a gift? For you look as
though you have hurt many and saved so few."

The swordsman confronts the old man, "How dare you? Do you
know how hard it is to govern steel, to fight ten men by
yourself and be victorious, well, do you? Old fool."

"I am sorry," he says, "I did not intend to enrage you, but it's true I
cannot fight one man, let alone ten men, not with an old body
like this."

The swordsman asks, "What's your gift? Come on, out with it."

The old man shows him his hands, "I can heal the sick, save the
wounded and bring back those an inch from death."

There's laughter and jeers from all the men as they shout, "Prove
it, let him prove it!"

"You had better prove it or I will run you through!"

With that the swordsman sees a young man trying to pass. He is
caught and held down, and in a flash he's fatally stabbed. The
old man limps forward, kneels down and places his hand on

the wound. He lifts the boy's head and whispers "I take your pain and your hurt and make it my own. May my love and inner soul remove the scars that you would bear and make you new."

There before all of them the young man stands, and he is healed and grateful. The old man stands but only just, as he struggles to his feet.

"Tell me old man, where did you get this gift, and will you share its secrets with me?" he asked.

The old man said, "My gift is the gift of loving words, that heal all who need it, but for every wound healed and a tear dried, I gain a scar. I was like you long ago when I was given this gift but I too am scarred."

With that he unties his robe and it falls to the dusty earth. His naked body is scarred all over, like a maze, so deep and coarse are the wounds that his soul can be seen shimmering.

"I see these are the scars of your battles. Why do you not heal yourself?"

The old man said, "This is a gift and a curse and it has a price. These are scars of the suffering that I have healed, every day my body is tormented by the deeds of others that I have had to endure in order to renew them."

The other men around him look on in horror; some weep and try to hide their tears.

One man steps forward and lays his sword at the old mans feet.

"You are more powerful than any army and our swords are weak against such a splendid gift."

He kisses his hand, they all follow suit and renounce their ways and each man leaves with a new sense of direction in life. The master swordsman is all that remains.

"Please give me the gift so that I may fight and slay many, and as my foes lay dying I will heal myself."

The old man tries to speak but a blade against his throat makes it impossible. He holds out his hands to a man who is blind and deaf to his own selfishness. He takes the man's hands that have caused much chaos.

"You wanted the gift of healing hands and I give it to you freely."

But there are two sides to every story. As the gift slips from his hands he says "I give you a beautiful gift and a cruel curse."

With that the old man glows and a wind passes through their bodies. As the brightness fades, the old man that was, is young again and scar free. But the swordsman is now old and tired and writhing in pain.

"What have done to me old man?" he cries.

"You asked for the gift, I gave it to you; now tell me, do you now need a new body?

For the gift I gave you is to heal others and not yourself. That is the price you pay for an amazing gift."

He leaves the now new, old man to heal others and to find forgiveness for all that he has done.

So I have to tell you, I may not be able to fight ten men, and I have no need to command an army of suffering .But what I can do, and what I will tell you is my words are stronger than steel. My passion for healing you will never rust. For we are all gifted with such words. If you are willing to listen, I am willing to heal you.

Show Time

There's a strange noise at
The end of the road,
Like the sound of cannons
A chaos that was foretold
People listened and looked
They stood in awe,
At a sea of oddities that passed down
By their doors
The way they walked and danced
Through the street,
Was like the flames of hell burning
At their feet
They jumped and laughed
And brought so much fun,
To a world that was dark, so heartless and numb
At the head of the parade there
Stood just one,
A man in a mask leading them on
He walked with hands
Down by his sides,
With a fiery passion
That burned in his eyes
A woman in the crowd called out
To the stranger
She asked "Who are you beings,
Such strange freaks of nature?"
The man in the mask
Started to grin,
For he knows of madness and a lifetime of sin
He told the woman "I am here with

My army and The Dark Arts,
We are here to set a fire
To ignite your hearts
For it seems to me that this place
Was once great,
As he called to the crowd
Follow me to Hells Gate"
The woman she spoke,
And she said,
"I recall a lost memory but they said you were dead!"
The man mask gifted her a smile,
Said "My good lady I was
In exile"
For there in the darkness and in
The cold shadows,
I cut the cruel noose where I hung from the gallows
But now I'm back and it's plain to see,
That you've forgotten good times
And almost forgot me
So let me set you at rest and put
Your mind at ease,
For me and my freaks
Are so eager to please
For I am an entertainer let me
Be your host,
I am alive, for I am no ghost
Now with the magic that
Has been restored,
Let me do what I can to
Keep you all from being bored
So the masked man and his
Freaks flowed down the road,
With a cry in the air I shouted
"Let's begin the freak show"

The Scientist

I met a scientist long ago. He made so many potions and
   wonderful contraptions and wore a pocket watch. I said
"That's a lovely pocket watch, wherever did you get it?"
He said
"It was a gift from a woman long ago. And now young man, how
   can I help you, for you seem to be looking for something"
"I am"
"What is it you need?"
I sat with him and asked about numbers.
"Can you tell me Sir, what are the chances of finding love a
   second time around?" "Hmmmmmm, that is a very hard
   question my lad, one that cannot be answered by numbers
   alone"
I sat and sighed
"I had it once; it was more powerful than a storm. And yet warm
   and gentle as grass in the summer sun, it was amazing and I
   fear I will never have it again"
The scientist said
"You wish to have that love again and never waste a second in her
   arms?
"Oh yes, I should have told her how I felt, I didn't and if I had
   she'd have been at my side until I died"
"Wow" the scientist said
"Dear boy, I think I can help"
He took me to a large room and in the centre stood a huge
   machine
"What is it?"

"This is a time machine Son, I have never used it. For I believe it will work only once" "I don't understand"

"You wish to love again do you not? And to be with her again?"

"More than anything"

"Then step inside"

I climbed inside and the door locked behind me

"Hold on, you're in for an amazing journey. This time around make it count. And tell Tia that you love her"

I gazed at the man

"What did you say? I never told you her name?"

The scientist smiled

"You didn't have to, for I have been waiting for you. And we both loved her"

"I don't understand, who are you?"

He smiled and said

"Time will tell"

Then in flash, there I stood with my arms around my love I lost so long ago She smiled

"Where have you been? I have been waiting for so long"

I kissed her lips

"It doesn't matter; I am here now and will never leave. And I love you today and forever. I love you till time stops"

And as we walked into the setting sun she gave me a gift

"Here, so you're never late again"

I looked and it was a pocket watch. And in that moment I knew, the old man that had solved time and space had also shown me love again. For time is all we have and I don't waste it. For science cannot explain a kiss, it's not science, it's magic

My Dark Friend

I have a dark friend who's
Always with me,
I'd give him all my money
If he'd just let me be
I'd say farewell, so long and take care
But he'll stay forever
His shadow I must bear
He takes me to places that
Are far away,
I wish he'd leave
But he's here to stay
He makes me walk until my
Bones start to ache,
Dragging me along 'til my
Mind starts to break
Walking the streets of a place
Called London,
These emotions I have,
You'll find in a dungeon
He strips me naked and has me
Crawling on the ground,
Screaming in agony I wish
You'd put me down
Shouting and screaming you leave
Me in pain,
While you dance all around
Calling me names

He said he was sorry and gave me
Many gifts,
To make me feel loved, to heal our rift
I took these treasures and
Learned them well,
But didn't know the cost was a price
Paid in hell
He said "I'll give you these gifts
And many will say,
That you're stunning, amazing, even magical today
You'll write many stories and
Warm many hearts,
But my dear boy you'll remain in the dark
For I'll let you smile and help
Many others,
But you're a lost cause like bones
Wrapped in covers"
I have to admit and I don't
Disagree,
That this dark friend will never
Leave me
But all is not lost and lest I forget,
This dark friend of mine
Hasn't beaten me yet
For when he crushes my bones
And pounds me heartless,
I refuse to yield
In the icy cold darkness
I said "You gave me these gifts
And poisoned my mind,
But my dark friend, you're no
Friend of mine
So now you know but
You don't clearly see,

What my dark friend has done to me
He makes me speak in a strange way,
Has you all asking
How do I write this way
And I'll reply "It's a blessing and many
Curses,
To be able to write these
Heartfelt verse's"
But this is a high price and a cost
Indeed,
Don't fall foul and end up like me
For as I battle my dark friend
And the war rages on,
I hope some day my dark friend
Will be gone.

The Antiques Dealer

An old man I knew once was locking up his antiques shop late one
night. He switches off the lights and as he closes the door he is
struck from behind with a heavy blow to the head. His world
goes dark and he knows nothing more. When he wakes he is
tied to a chair and unable to move. As his senses return and his
vision sharpens he sees two men looking at him.

"Wakey, wakey! Had a nice sleep did we?" they say.

"What do you want?" demanded the old man.

"We know you got riches in the safe and we want them."

"Common crooks, that's all you are! I won't tell you where it is!"

With that they beat the man to a bloody mess.

"Enough, enough!" cries the old man, "Untie me and I will show
you."

They untie him and throw him to the ground like a rag doll. He
crawls on his hands and knees to the safe and opens it.

"Take what you want but on your own heads and souls be it." says
the old man.

One man takes a watch and the other a book and a solid gold
chain.

"Take what you want but please leave the book, for I am also an
illustrator and haven't finished my sketches in it."

The men say "Must be worth something as it's in the safe."

The old man begs them to leave the book and tries to fight back
but is overpowered and beaten to within an inch of life. He
begs for mercy but kicks and punches continue to rain down
upon him.

"You fools you don't know what you have gone and done, you

know nothing of the wealth and power of the written word," he gasps.

The men take what their pockets can carry and set the shop on fire with the old man inside.

One year later, to the day the same two men are sitting in a tavern drinking and making fools of themselves. One of them gets up, shakes the others hand and leaves. He stands out in the cold of the night and makes his way to an alleyway to relieve himself.

"Excuse me," said a man. "Do you have a light?"

The man fixing himself replies, "Give me a moment old chap, too much ale I've gone and had."

The man turns, takes out his matches and strikes one up.

"There you go" he says.

Eyes glare at him from behind the small candle-like flame. The man's eyes grow wide and fixed and he recoils in shock. "You! It's you we killed! You old man, what evilness is this?"

"Evilness" said the old man, "Oh come boy, is it just to beat an old man? Take what's not yours, burn my shop and leave me for dead? But to come back from the dead is evil? What a strange way to be! Where is the book you stole? I don't care for what else you took, just the book!"

The man said "I haven't got it! My friend has, nobody dared buy it!"

"Indeed" said the old man.

The man now turned and climbed a drainpipe, as he got halfway; he slipped and fell but was caught by a solid gold chain around his neck that got hooked on a bolt sticking out.

'Snap' went his neck and death claimed him.

The second man, now drunk, picked up his sack and left the tavern. He wandered halfway down the street when he was stopped.

"Have you the time, dear sir? "

The half drunk man looked, but couldn't tell due to too much ale in his body.

28

"That's a nice watch, where did you get it, as I had one just like
    it."
The man looked and said "What's it to you where I got it? Mind
    your own old man and get outta my way!"
The old man stopped him and said "You can go but I want the
    book you stole."
The man, looking puzzled said "What book you on about?"
"The same one you stole along with that watch from my shop!"
He then became sober in an instant. "Who are you?"
As the man came closer, he screamed "Oh Christ! Oh dear God
    save me, for I am plagued by ghosts!"
"Do you have the book? It's all I want and you can go."
"The book is worthless, I couldn't sell it" said the man.
"The book is of great value to my client, it is his book and it's
    unfinished. He is a very dear friend of mine."
The man, now terrified was muttering "God save me, God have
    mercy on my soul."
The old man said "You took things that don't belong to you and
    yet, you beg for mercy?"
"Who wrote the book?" asked the man.
As the old man was going to tell him, he ran off dropping his sack.
    He makes down the path and crosses the road. He then
    glances down at the watch but as he does so, he takes his eyes
    off the road and is mowed down by a horse drawn carriage,
    crushed under hooves and wheels.
The old man bends down and takes the book from the sack and
    steps out under a street light. The carriage comes to a grinding
    halt.
"Your book Sir, I said I would return it and I have."
A dark figure with a whispering voice said "So you did and so you
    have, thank you, for this is my life's work. The night is at an
    end, would you like a lift? I am going your way; and you have
    yet to finish the illustrations in my book."
The old man smiled "I do believe you're right."

And so, he stepped into the carriage and said "It's a lovely book, a work of dark arts at its best."

The voice of the stranger said "Here, you can keep it, as you will be with me for some time. Let me sign it for you."

And so I did.

"Thank you …? "

"My name is in the book old man, have a look."

"So it is my dear friend."

"HELL'S PREACHER".

Mother In The Park

A young girl and boy sit cradling themselves; like the way a
mother cradles her newborn baby. The tears roll down their
faces and journey down their legs as they rest their chins on
their knees.

A woman passing by walked over to the children that seem to be
lost. She sat down and held their hands; she had a kind gentle
face and they came to learn that she had the most caring heart
that they would come across. And with that she began to speak
the only way a mother knows how; that soft gentle tone that's
more amazing than a violin played at midnight.

"Dears, where is your mother? For all children need their
mother's love."

They replied "We have a mother but she is not here right now and
we feel a little lost."

She sighed gently.

"I too know that of which you speak. For when I was young, I too
was alone. I was taken in by what I'd hoped to be loved one."

They could hear in her voice times of hurt, moments of her own
wounds weeping before them that they could relate to on such
a personal level.

"Go on please; you have drawn us in like the short winter
evenings."

"In my childhood years I battled hard and tirelessly to be loved
unconditionally and sought refuge in my dreams. For I am a
dreamer."

"What did you dream of that saved you? Please tell us so that we
may dream those dreams."

She said "I dreamed of flying, I also saw love and me being a
mother, feeling life growing inside me, seeing them laugh, cry,
run and be the mother that I never had, see their lives unfold
and hope they love me and remember all I have said and done
for them."

The words of this mother were so touching that even the two felt
loved by her as she looked out across the park that seemed so
empty.

They asked "So did you get your dreams?"

She looks down and her smile is like a thousand kids playing in
the park without a care for problems in the world.

Her eyes shimmer; "Oh yes I did, I left home before I was 18,
such a tender age; still I joined the steel birds that soar into the
heavens and onto the edge of the sun. I fell in love and had
two amazing children and to this day I am so blessed to have
them. For being a mother is more magical than any spell a
Greek goddess can cast."

"And what of love then?"

"It came and faded like the green in the leaves of trees in autumn
that scatter these playing fields. I hope to find love again, I am
always looking but it never reveals itself. But I can hope it will
find its way to me. My children have grown up now and I
have grandchildren so I am truly blessed."

They both stand up and hug the mother that spoke so softly to
them.

"You are a wonderful mother and any child would feel loved and
safe in your arms."

They pull away, pausing for a moment and then both kiss her
forehead.

"Your children Catharine and Steve know that you love them; for
they are a part of you and you think and feel the same."

The mother's eyes fill up with golden tears; "How do you know
though, tell me, how could you possibly know their names?"

They said "We know because we are the essence of their

childhood and you loved us and continue to love us in a way that only a mother knows how. We wanted you to know that we are proud of you mum."

She weeps tears of joy as the two children walk away; as she looks on they both turn their heads, smile and wave and with a gust of wind that sends the leaves cascading around them they fade.

A mother's love is more than words
It's a richness that money can't buy.
And what's in a mother's heart
For her children
Is just too beautiful to describe with words

.

To Catharine & Steve
From a mother we wish we all had and the world needs more of.
From Christine Wooler.

Dana

She walks up the stairs like she has done countless times and
  sighs. There's a room that's painted in soft shades of pink and
  blue, a rocking horse in the corner that's as new as the day it
  was bought. A painting set with many colours and a lonesome
  brush.
And a mother that looks on at her daughter and her son.
She sits on the end of the bed kicking her legs back and forth as all
  children do.
Laughing and giggling as her mum tries to put her tiny red shoes
  on that have shiny brass buckles on them.
"Mummy we'll always be bestest of friends won't we?"
And her mother replies "I hope so darling. I'll always be here for
  you and the day will come when I will have to go far away but
  always know I am just a smile and memory away."
The smile slips from her daughters face and in sad voice she asks
  "But why Mummy? I won't be able to see you and who's
  going to dress me and read to me?"
As a tear trickles down her face her mother dries her eyes. She
  pulls up her socks and kisses her daughters golden head of
  hair.
"You know something princess, wherever Mummy is I will always
  be watching you"
And her little girl replies "Like an angel Mummy?"
"Yes like an angel watching over you, and when you're lost and
  you feel all alone I'll be there to keep you safe and loved so
  don't ever feel that I have left you both completely."
She scrunches up her nose and tickles her mother under the neck
  and they both laugh until their cheeks are bright red.

"Run along and play darling."

And so she hops off the bed and heads out into the garden where the sky is as blue as her eyes.

She has no father, for he left many years ago. But before he did he hurt them both in a way that's so painful, so unloved that words fail to even start or finish such a tale without an ocean of sorrow to be lost at sea or drowned in.

Her mother stands at the kitchen sink as the kettle boils and looks out and sees the shadow that's cast as her little girl sits and swings high into the air on the garden swing.

Her little brother, just a baby, let's out a cry and the mother picks him up. To soothe and ease him she lays him down and for a gentle moment he's peaceful. But then he bursts into tears, screaming and crying with the might of a thunderstorm. The father sitting there snaps and hits the tiny baby and shouts lyrics that no child should hear.

The mother rushes over and covers the baby, defending him with her own body. And with no heart and no soul, he punches and kicks her and she holds her swollen bundle of joy that's just barely five months old, growing in her tummy. There lying on the kitchen floor, a mother holds onto her only child, her son Tyler, just one year old.

The kettle boils and the high pitch whistling wakes her from her dream and a cruel nightmare. She looks out onto an old rusty garden swing, its little seat faded in colour from the sun and rain. A warm gentle hand touches her shoulder.

"Morning Mum I'm off to school now. I'll see you later."

As he kisses his mum and grabs a slice of toast and heads out the door. But before he leaves he says, "I saw her Mum, I saw her the other day sitting on the swing."

His mother turns and asks, "What did she look like?"

And he replies, "Just like you said Mum. She had blonde hair and blue eyes, and she's always here."

The mother recalls what she would have said to her daughter

Dana Renee had she not been taken before she even got the chance to know her mother. And the words she remembered were:

"You're only a smile and a memory away."

There are times in her life when she feels that her daughter is nearby. In a place far away but watching over her like a guardian angel. Giving her hope when she needs it and smiles when her world seems sad.

She's always there; you never have to look as she is also a part of you.

For my
Dear friend Tricia Dean

For an ocean of tears cannot fill
The void and emptiness
That you have for Dana, your precious
Long lost child
But know that at every sunset,
And at every sunrise
You'll see her shadow swing back and forth
Laughing and smiling and if you listen you'll hear her
Calling your name and telling you that
She loves you.

Cathy's Memories

A young lady sat and watched a man break in two. It left her
feeling hurt, sad and angry, knowing that all of the comfort she
could give would not mend his world, but she had to try for
she was kind and compassionate. He sat on a bench in the
garden watching the flowers swaying in the wind and in deep
thought. She sat beside him, held his hand and said, "Today is
different from yesterday isn't it?" as she handed him a tissue to
dry his eyes.

"Today is very different indeed, for yesterday was lost overnight
and even though we have words and deeds to speak of and to
do on this fine afternoon, all will be lost like the rain that falls
and dries on our skin, for it leaves no trace."

The young lady ached deeply at his words and wished to dampen
the fire that scorched his mind. She said, "I have seen many
days like yours, filled only with questions and turmoil and I
wish I had answers."

The old man said, "I know, but for me it is new and always will be
for people like me. I have a close woman in my life and she
can't stand the sight of me. I told her I loved her but she said
how can I love a stranger? Yet for over 60 years I have known
her and what memories I have of us. But things changed, she
can't stand the sight of me."

The young lady put her arm round him and kissed his cheek.

"I just want her back" he said, "But old age and its close friend
Time has taken that from us."

The young lady took the old man to a room where they both sat
looking on at his close friend that seemed to be sleeping.

"My dear Rose, I still adore you like the first time we met and I still remember that summer dress you wore while laughing in the long grass, I only wish you could see those moments like I do and have them back."

He walks over and places a chain around her neck with a locket on it. He kisses her and thanks the young lady for all she has done and leaves the room with great sadness.

The young lady strokes her hair and she wakes.

"My dear who was just here?" she asks.

"A good friend of yours and he has left you a gift."

She feels for the chain around her neck and her fingertips slide down and find a heart shaped locket. She opens it and inside is two photos, one on each side.

"Tell me Young Miss, what is your name again?"

"My name is Catherine" she says.

The old lady then asks, "Who's that in the pictures?"

"Oh Rose, you don't remember do you?"

She shakes her head and says, "No I don't, I haven't a clue?"

"That, Rose is you and that is your devoted husband" says the lady.

"But I don't have a husband do I?"

And Catherine smiles and says "You do Rose but today you can't recall such precious memories."

Time has a way of saving us and helping us
But for some it steals their memories like the sun fading a painting
On the wall
Its true colours lost and forgotten
And if we could restore those
Colours we would.

For Catherine Suddaby
You have chosen an amazing job

That few can do and endure
And I know for each memory lost
Is a day of kindness given by
You to those that truly need it.

A Cup Of Tears

It's that time again, and the school bell rings, the sound of
hurrying feet, the banging of doors and laughter echo through
the halls from the excitement that it's the weekend again.
She's off saying her goodbyes and waving to her friends as she
heads down the road,
Homebound. ...
There's such a big smile on her face for such a young girl and
she's the only one who knows why.
It's something that many of us have or have had; the pleasure of
having a dad. She gets home and drops her school bag to the
floor as she waits at the gate for her dad. She climbs on the
gate, swinging back and forth as she hears the faint sound of
his whistling as he comes up the path. Her eyes light up like
new stars just born in the night sky.
"What you doing out here young missy?" he says with grin.
"Waiting for you Dad, how was work today?"
And he replies as he pushes open the gate and she tries to hitch a
piggyback ride on his back
"Work is work love, it's there and we are here and now it's the
weekend."
"Dad can you teach me how to whistle?"
He says "Maybe if you're really good I might."
And both laughter and smiles are exchanged between them.
Weekends are fun away from the playground and the stresses of
work, He teaches her to whistle, and how to lay bricks,
amongst other things.
"My dear Emma, your whistling is improving, but as for your
cement mixing, I have a little more to teach you."

As she sits with her, hands and shoes'n'socks covered in cement they build a wall together.

"Dad can we go and see Grandad?" she asks as she wipes cement across her cheek.

"Well, if we are going to we had better get cleaned up, before your mum wrings both our necks."

Her mum works long hours but it's all laughs and giggling as they mop up. After that they go and visit her grandad.

"Hello Dad."

"Hello son, how are you?" They shake hands and hug.

"And Emma every time I see you, you have grown a little more."

"Granddad, Dad's taught me to whistle!"

And he says "Has he now? Well let's hear it then."

She plays out a light melody from her lips, and he claps. "Well done Emma!"

"Thank you Grandad!"

In time she comes to learn from them both. They have days out watching horse racing,, showing her how to pick the winning horse, fishing on warm Sunday afternoons is also a great pastime of theirs.

But like the stream that flows in one direction, so does life and time as it trickles by.

The young girl is now 21 and my, how the years pass by so quickly. But as they do, with laughter and joy, there also come tears and sadness hand in hand. As her and her brother's mother is rushed to hospital with the swiftest of speed, and they see their dad like never before, as the weight of his tears hang heavy in his soft eyes, until they overflow and awash his cheeks with sorrow and pain. She slips from this world into the next leaving the three of them to continue this life without her.

At the lowest points, she finds herself at the wheel, foot to the floor, veering off the road. Trying to end her pain from the loss that's inside of her. Sitting at the wheel in a ditch as the

41

rain thunders down, she breaks down in tears, her head against the wheel and her hands pounding at the dashboard and windows.

But the love and strength for her dad spur her on and with time she becomes stronger and wiser. And so Emma, her brother Nigel and her dad find comfort in each other in hard times and embrace joy when it crosses their path. For the three of them have a bond that's awe inspiring. And whatever life throws at her, her father is there with a few kind, gentle words:

"Have a cuppa tea, Em."

For Emma Ellis,
May your mother be proud
And may the love for your father continue to be unbreakable
For the strength we get from
Our mum and dad is
Strength that cannot be weighed or
Measured but
Felt and seen by those around us
Who we hold most dear
And sometimes, just sometimes
They too need a little strength
As we all do.

Verse For The Departed

We sat and talked
From dusk 'til dawn,
Cutting each other's wrist's
To our favourite song,
Listening to a melody that scared
Our hearts,
And chewing on razor blades blinded
By the dark
As the beat played out we
Clapped and laughed,
Spilling our souls
Like a passionate blood bath
We sang, we cried
And we felt so alone,
Tearing at our features
Right down to the bone,
I said "Give me a chance and let me change this tune"
Hoping we find happiness in our solitude
I sat and I wept for the song repeated
Feeling lost and broken
My soul defeated
But he said to me with a smile and a grin
"This my song , our sickening sin
For you must sing along,
You must listen clear
If you don't learn the chorus
You'll be drenched in fear"

I tapped my fingers to this music of madness,
Recalling lost loves and
Memories of sadness
The needle scratched as it sliced
Though the ridges
The sound it made was like hell
Burning bridges
Torment and pain was the name
Of this hit
I beckoned and screamed
To be chained and whipped
He said "Young man
What's up, what's wrong
Don't you like this music, it goes on and on"
I closed my eyes
And covered my ears
But he cut out my eyelids
And gnawed at my ears
I begged and pleaded and the melody ceased
For the sound of the silence,
I was now at peace
For the cuts that I bore had given birth,
For now all my blood
Lay soaked in the earth
I don't know the lyrics, I've forgotten
The lines,
But if you listen closely
I'm still alive
For this is no song for the
Faint hearted,
This is a verse, for the dear departed.

Captain

"You are not defined by the clothes you wear," I said to a man who
    was sleeping on the street as I stopped to shelter from the rain
    in a doorway that he called his bedroom.
I said, "Sorry sir, I didn't mean to wake you but the rain is harsh
    and I wish to stay dry."
He looked up and rubbed his eyes and said, "Thank you young
    man."
"What are you thanking me for?" I replied, and he sat up and said
    "You called me sir, even though I am a tramp, my clothes carry
    the dirt from many peoples' shoes and I smell like a corpse."
I knelt down and met his eyes at a level where we were both
    equal.
"I called you sir because a man is not defined by the clothes he
    wears, but by the wisdom and chapters of his life that he
    passes down to others."
He took off his white faded cap and held it to his chest and said,
    "You dear boy, see more than most. For in another life I
    captained a great battleship and sailed with the bravest of men.
    I stood side by side, watched many good men die and saw
    many evil men live."
I saw in his eyes a heaviness that made me ache at his misfortune.
"Good sir, many people pass you by and pretend they don't see
    you when in truth they do. They are just frightened at the
    thought of ending up in a doorway like yourself."
He looked up at the rain and the sky above and said, "Many nights
    I have laid here and I have been chased from corner to post by
    those that see me as a blight in their path."

We sat as people passed by and sitting there, I too became invisible
to them and felt for a single moment like he must feel.

"You are no less of a great man than those who have fancy suits
and briefcases. My good captain of yesterday, your clothes
don't define you, and those that view you in such a way have
poor perception of life and remain blind."

So I took from my jacket, my wallet and gave him all the money I
had.

"It's not much but may it feed you and put a new blanket on your
back rather than these newspapers you curl up in."

His hands trembled with warmth and thanks. He reached into his
bag that he used as his pillow, unwrapped an old cloth and said
to me, "Here, take this good lad, for I know you understand its
worth and meaning." And he gave me a shiny gold medal.

"Great sir I cannot take this from you, for I have not earned it like
you once did."

He staggered to his feet and I rose from his dusty world.

"I give you this medal in honour; not of the fallen or of those that
lived to tell of great deeds, but in honour that you can see the
best in those that appear to be less than worthy of kind acts,
and great words, than any casual man may see."

He pinned the medal on me then wiped a tear from my eyes and
saluted me. That was a moment that defined him: A captain, a
defender and a gentleman but above all else a human being of
great wealth. I shook his hand and stepped back into the rain
that now began to ease and to this day I still wear the medal
with pride. And when people ask me did I earn the right to
wear to it?

I say "No, but I wear it in honour and in memory of the captain
who saw in me what many fail to see."

The Voyage For Now

Two soul mates sit and bask in each others company, laughing and
enjoying the day as if it was their last. These two are as close as
the night sky and stars, that's how they can be found.

"You know I love you and that I am always here for you," he says
as he places his head on her shoulder. That's greeted with her
hand that holds his face.

"I know you are and I thank you for being my friend and soul
mate. But it's time for you to go."

And he knows this, for a life at sea is his work, on a battleship that
sails on sapphire waves, in full view of an ever watching sky. He
makes his way onboard and waves to her with a bursting smile
that's caught many ladies' eyes. He has that way with women.
A real charmer, stealing hearts with just a few whispers.

The ship sets sail and his voyage begins. But all great adventures
come to an end and he hears the words, "Set sail boys, we're
heading home!" It's met by a cheering roar from the crew as
they punch the air.

"I'm coming home for my birthday and I can't wait to see you" he
said.

As his words are carried on the wind to her ears, she sits at home
on a distant shore she smiles and says, "I'll see you soon."

The day comes and his ship docks, he shakes the hands of his
crew. "See you soon, for when we next meet we will sail on
the Ark Royal."

Again they cheer. He steps down and touches land and she's
waiting for him.

"I missed you," she said "And I'm glad your home safe."

They head home laughing and talking about memory lane and how much fun they had growing up.

"I am going to be sailing on the Ark Royal and I can't wait to step aboard her deck," he said.

"I'm so proud of you, watching your dreams come to life, and it's your birthday."

"I know," he said "I have saved long and hard for on the waves, I have the ship to carry me, but on land I have just my feet, so I think I will treat myself."

He does, he buys his dream and sits there in it smiling like a big kid. A voice shouts, "She ain't no battleship!" as she laughs and smiles.

"That's true she ain't but she is a thing of beauty nonetheless," he tells her.

He gets out and she looks at him. "You're a little nervous aren't you? I can always tell and feel it, just like when I know you're coming home."

"I am," he said "It's the Ark Royal, an amazing ship, and a dream come true."

She replies, "You'll be fine, trust me, it's getting late they'll be waiting for you at the base."

And so they say their goodbyes and part. As she sleeps she hears his voice.

"Hey Sis, this is going to be my final voyage, I'm going to new uncharted waters. I sail on golden calm waves. My ship has set sail and these waters are under your skies, I know you worry for me and you always said that you'd be there for me. I just wish I could do the same for you."

But sadly this is a bittersweet truth that becomes true. He never made it to the base where he served in the navy just one week short of setting sail on his dream the Ark Royal; this amazing young man's life is cut short at the tender age of just 25 years old. For his journey back to the navy base was to be his last on this wonderful earth.

For Michelle Collins. Your brother would have been 36 today.

Losing a brother breaks your heart
And the tears you cry can fill an ocean and raise any lost ship from
    under the waves But with time and love
The waters become calm again.

In memory of Jason Campbell 5/9/1975 – 31/10/2001

On this your 36th birthday, May you sail on calm seas
And that one day your ship will reach ashore
And that you welcome Michelle aboard
But until then
May your voyage be gentle
And the winds guide you into the sunset.

David

How does a father tell his son to be strong when he is too weak
for words? And please tell me how does a son ask his father to
stay, knowing that it's selfish to ask him to linger a little
longer?
Could you? And if so when will the hollowness ever be filled
please? As I don't know how.
I knew a man some time ago. He was well liked and loved by all
who knew him. He had a life like so many that grace this
gift we call life. He had such a way with people that they
wanted to be by his side, to feel wanted. The way he spoke
and a smile that broke any storm clouds that might gather.
But all the friends in the world cannot and could not save
him. For the woman who loved him and bore his children
had found another. And this was to be the beginning of the
end.
His son watches as his world crumbles like a cliff reclaimed by the
sea.
His son tries hard to hold his fathers broken world together.
"Dad don't give up, there is hope still, don't let that fire burn out."
But the words are too late. For the inferno that once raged has
been dampened by the poison that dwells in a bottle.
"Son, it is too late, I am in its grip and it will never let me go. My
future is set in stone like that of a headstone on my grave."
The son weeps for his father as he descends into a dark place
where light is forbidden.
"Don't give in to it Dad."
His friends leave him with no outstretched hand for help and his

family disown him to the demon that now rapes his heart and soul.

Days become a blur and years roll by until a decade is on the horizon and all this time the son stays the course. Going the distance that others won't travel and now they sit in a park looking out on life where they have sat many times.

"Son there will be times of hardship in your life."

The son looks at his father and sees how life's wars have left this once sparkling being in such turmoil and sadness.

"You will have your heart broken many times, you will despair and lose control and break down and cry. And yes, you will lose many friends and loved ones and long for their laughter."

And as the son sits and listens, he feels the ocean of guilt drown him like the poison that has ravaged his father.

"Dad, I am sorry if I did not battle hard enough. I look at you and a part of me is dying."

"All must die and be no more son, but it's your choices that define you. For the choices you take will dictate the life you will lead."

A gentle wind blows and they sit side by side.

"My dear boy, ten years lost in wilderness and for what? Where did my life go? Don't you waste yours. For life's answers you won't find at the bottom of a glass."

The son turns away and wipes his tears, but this is no fairy tale and the ending is far from beautiful. Now the father lays in bed with curtains closed and a pale light flickers.

And a son who looks grim now faces a darkness with no candle to light the way.

"Dad, I am sorry for your life. I have not the words and you have not the time to listen to my story of forgiveness."

The old man reaches out his hand.

"Don't cry son, for all the tears cannot save me and I don't want to live any more. I am in pain and I am truly sorry that you must sit here and watch me wither away."

It's torture for the mind and loving heart. The son breaks down
and then recalls every memory, every hand shake, hug and kiss
his father gave him.
"Dad I ask you for forgiveness. I am sorry. When the time comes
and death wraps you in her arms, please go. I want you stay
but I know you want to go. Let death take you and set your
body at ease for evermore."
The son stands and kisses his father.
"I will see you tomorrow for sure."
As I leave the room I look one last time, he smiles and gives me
the thumbs up, but we both know that's the last time we will
gaze at each other.
As the door closes behind me and I step out into the cold winter
chill of a December's night, I look up at his bedroom window
and say my goodbyes.

So how do you let someone go?
When do you say goodbye?
And what if you're too late?
For some, saying goodbye is like shaking hands
And for others it's a smile and a thumbs up.

For I miss that old man,
I miss you Dad.

By The Bridge

The bell rings and many weary men's voices can be heard
shouting in delight as they finish for the working week. Many
machines slowly wind down and the dust settles as they finish
sweeping up.

Bending low to the sink, he washes his tired face and hands that
have borne the brunt of long hours labouring, His worn out t-
shirt clings to his body like a second skin as he cools the
stinging sweat on the back of his neck. Stepping out into the
summer's evening, he makes his way home with just one
thought on his mind. He smiles, it's a smile that all fathers
have; it's the anticipation of seeing his son and daughter at the
end of the day that urges him on home quicker and for a man
of his stature, he can move at a swift pace considering.

"Hello son" says a voice that's tired but not beat, as he close's the
door behind him.

"Evening Dad, hard day?" says his son as he takes his work bag
from him.

And his dad replies "Yes son, but less about my day, what of you
and your sister, staying out of trouble I hope?"

His son looks up and with an expression that's transparent.

He says "Yeah, of course Dad."

"Yeah right," his dad replies looking at him and nodding his head,
recalling his younger youthful self and all he got up to and got
away with.

"You know what tomorrow is son?"

His son's eyes widen and he bursts forward and says, "Fishing
down at Des Moines river??"

"That's the one son, so make sure you have yours and your sister's rods and nets ready."

His son jumps up'n'down and punches the air; an excitement that I hope we all have felt at some point in our lives but maybe we have lost a little of.

Summers are great as he raises them both by himself. The three of them fishing at their favourite spot on the river, learning to swim, and lessons in life he teaches them, which will guide them when the hard times come. Every year he takes them to Mako Kata caves where they run through the caverns and as the sounds of laughter echo back and forth, he watches on and wants these moments and memories to remain. There's a deep ravine that plunges down where time has carved its name into the jagged rocky face. High above is a bridge

"Come on you two, we gotta cross the bridge."

He lets them pass but they already know what's going to happen. Laughing and screaming they both reach the middle as their father shakes and rocks the old rickety bridge.

"More Dad, more!" cheers his son as his daughter holds on, a little scared but still giggling.

They sit out on rocks high in the heavens overlooking the range,

"Dad will days always be like these, I mean always so fun and magical?"

His dad sips tea from his flask and looks onto the horizon.

"Son, there will be many days like this, many more to be had. But you see that old bridge?"

And his son and daughter glance over at it.

And she replies, "Yes, what about it Dad?"

He places each arm around them.

"Life is like that old rickety bridge, it seems sturdy at first. Then as you continue, it becomes more uncertain and scary even. But as you reach the other side, it becomes safe again and if you look back at it, you'll see just how far you've come in life."

They sit, the three of them watching the sun go down.

The years tick by, moving from place to place, and everywhere is
    called home.

But just like that old bridge which becomes weaker with time, so
    does their rock. Their father becomes older and even wiser.

While sitting with his son and daughter, his son says, "Dad, we're
    planning a family reunion, everyone's going to be there."

His daughter sits holding his hand. "All of us together, it's
    something we've all wanted for so long."

Their dad looks at them with eyes that hold many stories, but this
    is a story that they don't see or read.

"You both go, I need to rest, I'll be here when you get back."

They hug their father, not knowing that it would be their last. He
    let's them go, and as they leave to make their journey he says,
    "Aric, Dawn, remember the bridge, remember it always,
    remember how far you've come."

And both reply, "We will Dad, we will let you get some rest."

They leave to make their journey and as the door close's and they
    set off, he leaves to make his final journey across that bridge
    where he can look down on them both and be truly proud.

Gayle

It's the afternoon, butterflies can been seen fluttering as they
nestle on flowers and dragonflies make haste over the waters
edge. This is where a shy child can be found dipping her toes
into a pond and dropping small stones into the water as the
ripples play out across the surface. She giggles as the fish
nibble at her tiny toes "Granddad," she asks "Do you think
fish have brothers and sisters?"
And her Granddad laughs warmly. "I guess so, little one."
"I wish I had a sister, but how do the fish know who's who? They
all look the same," she replies as she looks up and squints at
her Granddad with the sun shining on her face.
"They just know darling, they have that special feeling and they
know."
She looks down at the fish and as they come up for air, trying to
touch them; she falls in, soaking her Sunday dress. Her
Granddad, wearing his Sunday best clothes, wades in after her.
"You and me are for the chop now little one, wait 'til your
Grandmother sees us, she'll feed us to the fishes."
The little girl climbs onto his back and laughs at the unexpected
fun they've had. The telling off they get from her
grandmother is well worth getting mucky for.
She loves spending time with her Granddad as he teaches her
about animals and plants in his garden and of the microscopic
world beneath her feet. It's when she feels most happy, But
there is one who does not share or care for her world. A child
that loves her mother but her love is received with a cold heart
and an empty smile. It's a sad world when a child fails to

connect with her mother through no fault of their own, and the parent shuns them away to a darkened corner. Many times she has a strange feeling that she's not alone, that there's a lost shadow waiting to be found. Like the shadows that hide behind fallen trees in a forest. So she asks her mother about a girl named "Gayle" who was mentioned for a fleeting moment. Wanting to know if it's real, what she thinks and feels, like those small fish. But the reply is swift and sore; a beating is all that's given to her in answer of her question. Time and time again she asks and the physical answers she's given are forever the same. Cold cruel words are just as painful as any blow that can be landed and felt.

Time passes and the child grows and she changes shape. Moving through life on a rocky bricked path, but the shadow that she seeks still remains in her mind.

She loses her close friend, her Granddad. He's lost and overcome by darkness that many of us will sadly see and touch at some point in our lives. And the connection between her and her mother is all but gone, resenting the very air that her daughter breathes.

Now a thirty one year old woman, she looks for a woman named Gayle, using special places that relink and rekindle old past times and friendship. It's here at this point where crossroads meet, where deeds of the past hidden from eyes are found and discovered.

For the child, now a woman learns she's not alone, for the wickedness of her mother runs deeper than the roots of an oak tree. She learns that there was once a child that stepped in her path before she was born. And that child was left on a doorstep with a note with pointless words from a hollow soul that gave her up. But crossroads do meet, just like the tide reaching a sandy shore. Now there are not one but two shadows. Two sisters, who despite all the odds and the years of distance are closer than any shadow you'll ever find. The connection is far greater than that of their mother's. The missing link come full circle; they speak and talk like friends of old, like a book that's found its cover they fit perfectly together. And even though they have not met in person, I am sure the time will come when they will both sit with their feet in a pond, at the water's edge.

Once more.

For Mhairi Goodwin & Gayle

Two sisters
Who found each other in a world
That's far from perfect
For the love of a sister is
More personal and precious
Than any painting or treasure
It's a connection
That's felt between two souls
No matter how far it
May be or the distance
Of time
A sister is not a shadow
Or a lost hope
But a best friend
Priceless and timeless
And may we all wish
For such a great gift.

The Blinding Flames

In a cave, in a place
So far from here,
In a chamber of horrors that
That was stained in fear
I met an old lady
Chained in the dark,
Who had no eyes and a distasteful
Heart
She hung from the walls,
Shackled in chains, screaming
Cursing, enjoying the pain,
She had many cuts
Right down to the bone,
That shone in the shadows, so she wasn't alone
I asked the woman who
Was shackled and tied,
"What is this madness , where are your eyes?"
She coughed and croaked and she
Let out a cry
"You repulsive being , you disgusting child
I cut out my eyes and loved the feeling,
For lust and desire
Now it's just infected healing
I hated the thought of looking at you,
You made me feel sick,
If only you knew"
She thrashed and withered

And spat in my face,
She said "You're weak, you're human, a terrible mistake"
I stepped back and felt crushed
Inside,
At these cold hearted words
That made my soul cry
I said to this creature
That spouted hate,
"You belong in this darkness
This is your deserving fate
It was not lust, it wasn't desire,
That made you tear out your eyes
Your love for me, it
Seems to have expired"
She laughed and screeched
The echoes ran deep,
A promise by a mother
She failed to keep
"I came here looking for peace of mind,
To complete the puzzle ,
Understand the torment inside
But all I've found
Is gloom and despair,
These emotions you have
Have you imprisoned here.
The woman howled
"Be gone, dear child
For I care not,
The memory of you
Has started to rot,
You're nothing, you're worthless
Like the cursed earth,
Should have seized the moment
And drowned you at birth"

I looked at the flames
As they died down,
Something so evil cannot be laid in the ground,
"I grow tired of your empty heart,
So I'll grant you
A last gift, a friend in the dark,
You need no eyes to see his face,
You'll feel his touch
A warming embrace"
Here he is
And he has many names
I walked away
And she went up in flames.

A Day Like This

I sat and talked
To marble and stone,
Wishing it was possible
To call you on the phone
To hear that voice
So gentle and clear,
But instead I keep pretending
That you're still here
Laying down flowers in a place
You shouldn't be,
But when the bell tolled
You went and left me
To a distant place
So far away,
You gave your word you'd always stay
He said to me on a day such
As this,
"There will come a time when
I'm sorely missed
For all sons must know
And need to understand,
Life is too short
Time waits for no man
Leave your mark
For the world to see,
So when you fade
You leave a legacy"

At the time I wasn't
So sure,
For these words he spoke
I kindly ignored
So I replied to my dad ,
Who sat with a beer,
"You are strange, old man
You act as though you're
Not here
You talk as if you're leaving
My side,
Can you explain what you mean
This secret you hide?
For you told me
On a day such as this,
You'll be gone
One day and be sorely missed
I don't understand
And you talk in riddles,"
Then I looked at his face
And I was torn down the middle
He raised his head
And said with a gasp,
"You can't sit here
And linger in the past,
For you said you
Were sorry far too many times,
It's time to let me go
You've committed no crime"
The old man was right
And I knew what he said,
As I sat there
Whispering, talking to the dead
He said

"Lay down those weights
And unshackle those chains,
I have to go now,
No more time to explain
Just do what you can
And create something real,
Use your gift of words
Use them to heal"
And so for those of us
We kiss their stones and
We walk away,
And I wish you all
A Happy Fathers Day.

In memory of
David C. Webb
20/8/1941 – 7/12/2007
R.I.P
As it says on your stone
Old Man

"Sadly missed
But
Remembered with a smile"
Always.

Stepping Stones

She's a shy child. The way she talks fast, stumbles over her words
when she's nervous and picks at her fingertips to keep herself
calm. Like all children she's full of life and play, Animals and
the great outdoors have her in such a world of amazement and
questions, which she instantly wants to know the answers to.
And when she is given them, she asks that all important
question that all kids do, "But why?"

She loves riding her bike fast down a hill, trying to catch her
breath and then climbing back up the hill to do it all again for
just a few moments of laughter, as I am sure we have all done
at that age.

Her dark brown hair flows past her shoulders and it swishes from
the twists and turns as she does her ballet dancing in the
afternoon, her mother and father both smile and clap.

"Look Mummy, look at me! Watch what I can do!"

She spins with the ease and grace of a swan and never tumbles or
loses her footing.

Weekends are spent at the beach and by the lake where she tries to
skip stones across the water with her mother while her father
is hard at work.

"Darling, hold the stone softly in your fingertips and then whip
your hand back'n' forward," said her mother.

She tries, but the stone sinks to the bottom. "I can't do it mummy,
why can't I?"

Her mother sits her on her knee and says, "It takes time and
practice, don't be in a rush to do or learn anything, take your
time."

The shy girl picks up two stones, tapping them together and says, "I want to be grown up like you Mummy, I want to be a little big grown up and have a baby of my own."

Her mother chuckles at her warm words and says, "And you will, all in good time. You are far too young to worry and see what we grown ups have to face."

"Yeah but I can ride my bike faster than you and Daddy," she says.

Her mother picks her up and carries her to the car; they get in and head for home.

"What's the rush Mummy, are we late?"

Her mother replies in an excited voice, "Guess who's coming to stay honey?"

The child looks up and her finger pokes her cheek as she ponders, "Is it Father Christmas?"

Her mother bursts into laughter that makes her daughter giggle as well.

"No Silly, your uncle is coming to stay. He's finished fighting in the War and he's going to be living with us all."

Then they get home and, there, on the doorstep is her uncle.

"Hello you, I've heard all about you."

He greets his sister and her daughter and they head inside. The girl hears of stories of bravery and tears as she asks her uncle what it was like fighting.

"Don't tell her Hun, about your days in that place, she's too young to know or understand what's out there in the big world," says her mother who has already seen and read of the horrors of war.

But unknown to her mother and her father, her brother is a monster, a beast, less than an animal. For the pain and wickedness he has been inflicting on this young child without her parents' knowing is nothing short of heartbreaking and life changing. These are acts that only adults should know of, not for poor helpless children that have small voices.

Years go by and in time the sick cruel acts of a so called loved one are finally discovered and the truth revealed. Caged like the vermin he is, he's locked away and the child can start to feel alive and skip stones again. She learns to play the piano and plays as people sing. They look on at this beautiful being, never knowing what she has endured in her early years! But she smiles and beams like the morning sun's rays.

Many years pass and she devotes her life to helping and saving others and sick animals. She works long hours but she knows she is making a difference.

The young girl, now a woman sits on her balcony with rain to keep her company, and her view is no less stunning than that lake she skipped stones across. Tall trees and mountains are her view, and as the mist rolls in across its peaks, it's matched by the sound of children splashing in puddles left by the day's autumn rain.

As she watches on and listens, she wonders deep down in her heart if she can and will ever be able to have children of her own. If they will ask questions and be able to dance with ease and great grace through this wonderful gift that's called Life, like she should have been able to do.

Only time will tell if her one wish will come true.

For Loria Warren.

I hope the day will come when
You will look down
From your balcony
And see your child playing in the puddles
And may you skip many stones together
Across a lake that's as calm and clear as life can gift you.

67

Distant Shores

Sitting on the sofa, she watches all her favourite cartoons,
laughing away in her world of wonderment and magic. Her
cat looks puzzled by her actions as her fingers point at the TV
and she giggles to herself. The shy child doesn't have many
friends to talk to, but the friends she does have are just as
dazzling as her smile: a cat called TJ, a hamster, a small turtle
and a dog named Yoda.

The long hot summer days are spent playing with what few
friends she has and her dog. She misses her mum a lot, as she
puts in the hours working trying to earn her degree.

"Mum, can we go out later even for just an hour?"

And her mum replies, "Hun, your mum is tired; I got a shift to
work. You know money is tight and I need all the hours I can
get."

Her daughter sighs and looks to the ground for a hug that she
doesn't get. There are many days like this when she wants and
longs for love as her father is away in a distant place, fighting
his own loneliness and troubles.

She heads outside and sits in the afternoon haze of the clammy
warm air with her companion.

"Oh Yoda, at least I got you old boy," as she hugs him he licks her
face, with his floppy ears catching her rosy cheeks.

"Yoda your ears are so floppy and that's how you got your name."

She smiles as her dog rests his head on her lap and looks up at her
with those innocent eyes that can melt the hardest of hearts.

School isn't much fun as the child is picked on and mistreated by
those that are cruel, all because of the hand-me-down clothes

that her mum can afford. She heads home, skipping along as her hair bounces up'n'down with her bag hanging off her tiny shoulders.

As she crosses the road to her house, she sees her dog and he gets loose and runs towards her…

There is a silence so painful and harsh; it could break your heart if ever you heard it. The poor dog is hit by a car as the child watches his lifeless body flung to the ground. A moment that no caring eyes should see, her eyes stream with crystal tears as she sits with her companion stroking his ears and whispering, "It should have been me boy, it should have been me."

Sadly the dog passes away and with him so does a fragment of her heart, forever tainted by hurt and loss of her beloved dog.

Life deals many cards, and not always the best of hands are dealt kindly enough. For the Queen of hearts is what she needs and the King of hearts to make her feel wanted and loved.

They move house and in her high school years she opens up a little and gains some friends. Her mum married a man that was just a loser, a nobody, and she slowly starts to forget about her daughter. So she herself seeks love and finds it with her high school sweetheart, a way to find happiness and feel wanted but also a means of escape.

For those that don't know, love like that fades faster than any sunset you will have ever seen. Now she's a young woman looking for love that lasts longer than a season or than a flower dying from the autumn chill.

She makes mistakes, as we all have done, but few lessons are learned as she has her heart and body broken time and time again by others that leave her empty, and have taken her children from her.

Sitting here now, a woman who has seen and felt many hardships along the way, she finds love. In a far distant land in the most unlikely of places, where the hills are a lush green, the valley's bursting with life and the air is crisp and sharp.

She crosses a great ocean to find her love and even though they
have spoken and sung of this moment, never in their dreams
did they think that love could span so far and be so warm and
real. They go on to marry, and have a wonderful daughter, but
in time she longs for home and her husband wants a great
adventure.

And so the story ends with her love, life and family coming full
circle. The three of them board a plane for her long lost home,
where they settle. It's tough but with love and support she
regains her children.

Sitting there the little daughter's father brings home a small puppy
that chases his tail in a circle, flaps his ears and the little girl
asks, "Mummy what should we call him?"

With a fond smile and a tender memory she says, "What about
Yoda?"

With that they head inside to a house and a home filled with love.

For my dear friend
You travelled many miles to
Find a life filled with love
And I hope it lasts
Longer than any sunset
Or oak tree
That can be seen or found
In this world
Or the next
For that is what we all long for
Just a piece of love
And someone to give it to
And to share life with
May your journey and the journey
Of others be amazing.

Call Of The Wild

I saw a hunter and his son sat by the camp fire warming their cold
hands, which were colder than the dead of night that
surrounded them. I listened as he told of tales of hunting wild
animals and the lust that poured from their lips was as hollow
as the man himself who spoke them.

The son asked his father, "Father why do we hunt these animals as
if they are beasts from an evil place that time has forgotten?"

"We do it because we can, for sport and the thrill of the chase," the
father said.

The son's face looked troubled and unsure of what he felt, a part
of him torn in two.

"In the morning we will track the beast and you will see that these
aren't magical creatures but vermin."

The fire dies down and the embers glow in the still, icy air. As
they drift into a deep sleep I move from the shadows that have
kept me hidden and I thank her, The Darkness, which engulfs
my naked body, yet clothes me from all seeing eyes. I never
travel alone; we move as a pack, silently at night. We have a
bond that few will ever see, let alone have.

We leave the two untouched and move back into darker places that
you can't view or know of. We huddle together for comfort
and warmth as the wind howls outside like many songs that
we have sung on countless nights like this.

Even though I am different, I am loved all the same despite my
features which would frighten my family.

The next day, the father and son are tracking us like a hungry pack
with lack of purpose and love but intent on sheer

heartlessness. My mother and father wake me and sigh ever so gently, their eyes pale blue holding me in a trance. As we leave, a sound of thunder breaks the silent dawn.

"There they are son, now today you become a man! Raise your gun and fire, Damn you!" the father's coarse voice demands, yet the son pauses and sees a sight that has him almost speechless.

"No Father, leave them, let them go, please. I think I saw a young man."

But he is cut short, the father's fury is swift and he aims the gun at him.

"Now, Damn you!" he cries, "Pick up your gun and shoot! I've hunted this pack most of my life and have never been so close to victory!"

The son looks at his father like he's a stranger. "No, no I can't; I won't do it. Don't you see this is wrong? They belong here, we don't."

His father aims the gun and again the stillness is shattered but he doesn't shoot his son. He shoots a wolf and as the bullet finds its target, I stop and see my mother crash and plummet to the ground. She lays there motionless, unable to move. Our heads brush together and I crouch but it's too late, as her pale eyes grow paler than the snow that's now her last bed of an endless sleep. I stroke her one last time as my fingertips feel her grow cold and as I weep my tears fall and freeze like pearls. Instantly my pack is scattered and I'm alone.

I watch from afar as the father drags my mother away for his own twisted pleasure, but the son sits as the pain sets in because of what they have done, cutting him in two like the cold gnawing at his knuckles. As he leaves his father, he turns and says "You're wrong, they are not vermin, they are anything but. We are vermin and they are graceful, too graceful for us to understand."

The father sees something in his son, looks at the wolf at his feet and the shame of his actions eats away at him, like Time breaking down a mountain.

"You are right son; I am a blind monster that should be shot, not this amazing creature."

He buries both the guns and my mother in the snow. As they walk away, his father says to him, "So what was it you saw that had you speechless?"

He replies, "Nothing Father, I thought I saw something but I must have been wrong."

The father chuckles, "There was an old story long ago about how a boy was raised by wolves; can you believe that, wolves?"

His son said, "Imagine that, a boy raised by wolves; such tales are just too wondrous."

"Indeed son indeed."

As they continue to walk and the afternoon lingers on, a faint smile on the son's face tells the truth of what he saw.

I watch them leave my range I'm now moving alone, through the snowy rifts that sculpt the landscape.

We don't belong in their world, entering into their realm to steal such beauty from the wilderness when it's not ours to take.

For the day will come when a lone wolf is all that's left and how sad that makes my heart feel. How truly empty the world would be without the enchanting call of the wild.

The Fallen And Remembered

It's those words, and a place that every man here thinks of and
screams in their head. But few say it, although they all long for
it. For this is a place and time of despair, horror and where
hope is all but lost. They listen as those words are painfully
said by a terrified voice, "I want to go home."
Spoken by a young man who sat huddled and shaking in the
downpour of the rain.
"I just want to go home, for Gods sake, please, someone take me
home."
They all look on as this young fresh faced boy, barely a man, sits
on the edge of darkness; crying and in need of a warm
embrace.
The smoke and gunpowder rise in the air, in the cold of the night,
and the only light bestowed upon them is that of bright flashes
of bombs that are dropped on them from the heavens above.
The ground quakes and the smell of their fort in the deep muddy
trench is vulgar and bitter to their senses. As it burns and dries
their throats, they look on at this lad who should be at home,
starting out in life and having a family of his own.
"Have courage son," said a deep and lean voice that sat alone, away
from the others.
"How can I sir, when all I see is death? Knowing I'll never see
home again, I don't want to die. Not here. Not alone."
The captain laid down his rifle and walked through the mud that
stood almost knee high. He looked down on him with great
affection in a place where that does not belong, he kneeled
down and put his hands on the young man shoulders and said,

"Son, all men die, would you rather die knowing that you gave your life for the freedom of many? Or die having been selfish and cold for your own sake? You are not alone lad, we are here, and should the time come that I fall in battle remember me and my words."

The young man lowered his head from the grief that he felt.

"What's that sir?"

The captain took off his lifesaving helmet and told him, "Today I am free and from this moment on we defend the freedom of every man, woman and child back home. For if we fail, if we give up, then all of this is for nothing."

All the other men stood and came to the aid of their dear friend.

"Chin up lad, for the world will remember that we gave all we had to stop many that oppose us in our bid for freedom."

One of the men took from his war-torn bag, an old beat up and dented flask.

"Here lad, something to steady the nerves."

The young man knocked back a shot of brandy that warmed his chest and made him gasp. The men all cheered and for the smallest of moments you would have thought that they were in their local pub on a Sunday. But the moment passes and is shattered as the sound of gunfire tears through blackness.

"Get down boys, and hold your ground!"

As all the men dive for cover, holding onto their army helmets; the screams and cries of the wounded bellow in the darkened trench, as bodies crawl over each other for safety.

"No prisoners men, you hear me?" shouts the captain as they aim their guns and shoot shadowy figures that are advancing towards them.

Men who have been shot drag themselves to save others. As the young man picks up his rifle he watches as his fellow comrades use their bodies as shields to protect the wounded and dying. He catches his captain's gaze and sees he is pinned down by rapid fire. He turns and aims his rifle over the trench walls, breathes slowly and the sound around him becomes silent as he picks off four gunmen one by one, saving his captain from certain death.

The onslaught eases for now as they count their losses of ammo, but more importantly their men. It is no place for young eyes; there's no glitz and glamour in taking a life, and the deeds, however great, all carry a cost. The toll is heavy on such weary minds and souls.

It's late but early enough for the sun to rise and lift their spirits.

"Gentlemen we've made it through another night," said the captain who stood, watching Hell unfolding in the distance.

"Men, listen to me now, like you've never had to listen before."

The men look at their captain and they see in his eyes what they feel in their hearts.

"Men, today we are free, but to live another day as free men, I cannot promise."

He looks at the lad and draws a deep sigh, "Gentlemen pick up your rifles."

They do, knowing this will be their last stand.

"Men if we fall today, we fall as free men. May God save our souls."

They reload, outnumbered and low on ammo and stand together one last time.

"Lad you saved me before, and I am in your debt."

The lad now has a fire burning in his eyes, which he didn't have before.

"Sir, you'd give up your life for us, it's only right we do all we can to protect it."

The captain shakes all their hands.

"Men, for Queen and Country and for Freedom!"

They climb the deep, steep bank and see that this is their last stand. The captain whispers to the lad as they venture forward, on to certain death, "Nobody else I would have at my side when faced with death, dear boy."

The young man replies, "It's been a complete privilege sir, and an honour serving with you."

The two men and their friends give all they have as they go over the wall and on to the battlefield beyond. There amongst the mud and empty shell casings of bullets, the captain lies dying and the lad has not scratch on him.

"Sir you saved me!"

Indeed the captain did, covering the lad and taking the life stopping bullets into his body, saving him from certain death.

"Lad, let them know we gave our all, that we gave no ground."

With that, the young man hands him his rifle and he lays it on his chest.

"Yes sir, I will, you've given me hope, and the world freedom. For we won the battle and the war is over."

And with that he stands and salutes his captain as his eyes close and he slips away. He picks up his rifle, walks out of the gloom of the wasteland and looks back. To his amazement he sees the ghosts of his fallen friends, watching and cheering him and the captain saluting him. Slowly they fade as he walks away into a world filled with hope and freedom.

In memory of those that gave their lives for us so that we can be free.

We remember the heroes of yesterday
And keep them in our hearts always
The fallen, the brave, those that lived to tell of such sorrows and pain
We are forever in your debt.
Remembered now and forever more.

Fathers And Sons

On a stool I sat with a friend that I knew well. In his eyes I saw
trouble and great loss.

"What troubles your mind, my friend?"

He looks up from his dark world and says to me, "Today my heart
breaks and my world is at an end, I am falling."

"It pains me to see you like this, so broken and hollow, please tell
me why are we here."

He said, "I am losing something that's worth more than all the
riches in the earth. It's so amazing that it can't be painted, nor
can it be sung in a song to soothe my heart."

I sat and searched my nightmares for what could slay such a man's
feelings. I drew from my own life that which had almost killed
me and destroyed my perfect world. I sighed, "Say that it is
not so, say that what you are going to tell me is someone else's
nightmare?"

He sat, and as the background music played, it was in that
moment he was taken back to when his dad held him in his
hands like a teardrop from the sky, His eyes filled with
memories that swept down his face like a waterfall in a storm.

"My dear friend, I know what taints your heart, and my inner-self
aches for such a loss which you must endure."

He smiled, and that is a testament to his strength, for to smile
when there is no hope is more than any human can muster at
any time.

"My dear boy, I tell you this; when the waking hour comes, and
the walls close in, before his eyes close forever, say all you
need to. Recall every kiss, every time he stroked your head,

and when he said he'd always be there, he meant every word.
For great kings grow old, temples crumble and fall.
For in the end the love between father and son is one that is more
powerful than words. It is an understanding with a smile, or
the touch of a hand that says all you will ever need to know.
And know that when he slips away you are there to keep his
departed soul company."
My friend replied, "Thank you; it's been a while since I saw you
last and I thank you."
He stands and walks away to face a time in his life that will break
him, but knows that friends, whether new or old, are always
there to carry their heart when sorrow is too great to bear.
For the love for a friend is more endearing than any sunset.

For you my friend
I know that Dark Place
But I'm with you always.

Red

There was a woman I saw
In a distant crowd,
Her body had curves
Of unholy clouds
She walked with evil and darkness
At her side,
With a look on her face
"Come no closer or you will die."
The grin she possessed
Was hidden and real,
For entombed in her flesh was
Metal and steel
She knows of horror to the
Highest degree,
She'd slit your throat
To be happy and free
But this
Is no saint or a trick of the mind,
She'll murder your soul
And snap your spine
So here she is
And I hope you listen well
For the woman I saw
Was more beautiful than the
Catacombs of Hell.

Time

I had an amazing friend once; he was like no one I had ever met. I
    met him at a time
that's so far back I can't remember. Every day was new, special
    even. I lost count of
how many times he helped me, from making new friends, to
    travelling the world. He allowed me to love and be loved. He
    was splendid.
Then one day without warning, in a rage he sought to take from
    me all I had loved; friends, family and even a loved one. He
    snatched back all my memories and left me in limbo. In his
    wake he destroyed everything around me.
I asked him, "Why? How did I wrong you?"
He said in a calm gentle voice, "I am sorry my friend, but
    everything withers and dies and you are no exception."
My eyes wept and my heart fell with no sound.
He said, "I am sorry, but now you must fade as all magic does"
He dried my eyes and he took my hand, and I thanked him for my
    life, but as we walked away into the pale purple sky, I asked
    him, "All these years, you never told me your name?"
And he replied "I will tell you my name,
My name is "Time"
And with that I was nothing more.

Dear Dad

You made a mistake
At the start of your life and they took
From you
Your freedom
Kept you behind bricks and mortar,
But in your darkest moments
You never forgot
I was your daughter
In your heart you remained
Strong and true,
If only we had more time,
But in the end we never knew
Time passes so quickly
Like the ocean tides,
You've gone now,
But not forgotten
I know this is not goodbye
To Jenny, Jamie and Stuart our
Father still remains,
We'll meet him at the
End of time
Our memories will never fade
Dad, you have no time
It's time for you to go,
But I'll see you in a sunset sky
This I truly know.

Reunited

This is where we leave you
Sleeping
Safe and sound,
Listening to the birds as we
Lay you down
Your life was filled with happiness
Running wild and in the park,
You've closed your eyes
You've gone now
But you're forever in our hearts
The way you used to look at us
So gentle without
A frown,
Your blanket has grown cold
For your heart no longer pounds.
Mornings are so sad,
And the days
They linger on,
A collar with no keeper
For you have drifted on.
When the nights draw in
And I feel I can't go on,
I'll remember all we shared
Our special unbroken bond
A keeper with no companion
No friend to dry my
Eyes,

This is your last sigh now
It's time
To say goodbye
Thank you my dear friend
You've given me so much,
We have laughed, danced and smiled
I'm longing for your touch
Now there is a silence
So painful and so clear
I wish you could use your paws
To wipe away my tears.
Please do not fret, do not sit and cry
For Sooty and Cai
Are now together
Running in the sky.

For Chris Wooler
In loving memory of
Your dog "Sooty"
May the parks in the sky
Welcome her
With endless love
And may Cai be waiting to greet you
Reunited in death
But sorely missed in life
We'll remember always
"Sooty"
2/7/1998 – 24/5/2013.

The Path

A man in old work clothes, working the soil and caring for the animals that graze upon it, stands before the dawn that stole the sky with its colours and a sun that warms the waking world. He continues to work into the afternoon, when a tiny shadow comes racing up the dusty path.

"Granddad, Granddad it's me!" shouts a voice that's so loud it's hard to believe it came from such a small flower.

"Oh my dear girl," he says.

As he kneels, she tumbles into his arms and they both fall back laughing.

"Oh little one, it's good to see you, what a wonderful surprise this is!"

As she cuddles him and beams of joy are exchanged, she says, "I've come to stay Granddad. For the holidays!"

"Oh you have, have you? Then let's not waste another minute." And they walk down the path hand in hand and head for home.

Weekends and holidays are great there, that's all she ever longed for, to spend time with her granddad as he'd tell her stories while he sat in his rocking chair or she'd sit on his lap and sing to him.

"You have the soft voice of an angel. May I live long enough to watch you grow and become proud of you," he tells her.

"I hope I do make you proud Granddad, one day," she says as he tickles her and she giggles.

They sit eating peas they picked that he grew in his allotment as they watch the day end and a new night is unveiled.

They both grow and move forward like we all must do. He works
on the railway, maintaining the trains; backbreaking work, but
his body is used to such labour. Yet still the little girl, now a
woman, comes running up the path calling for her granddad,
but this time it's extra special, as he's a great grandfather now.
"My word, how amazing and equally beautiful as your mother
you are Jemma."
She smiles; "Thank you Granddad"
Proud tears they all share, and all three hold hands and stroll
down that old path together.
"Me and your mother used to walk down this path when she was
just knee high, and here we are again; you, me and my great
granddaughter. I never thought the day would come, and it
has."
His granddaughter said "I can't believe we are here Granddad, and
I hope you are proud of me. You gave me so many memories
and a priceless childhood."
He smiles at them both, "Well, what you have given me has made
my life complete."
As he sits there in his rocking chair with Tracey and Jemma, he
knows that there will be another little girl who will wander up
that path.
But that is a dream he wishes to see, and sadly never got to fulfil;
for now he lays in a bed and time is short. His granddaughter
Tracey sits with him for what she knows will be the last time,
and she sings the song she sang so long ago to him as that
bittersweet moment comes, and he walks down that old path
one last time to the laughter of his grandchildren.

In memory of Richard Isaac 1/10/1902 – 11/6/1988

Memories are etched within us
'Til the very end

And sometimes what we want
Is just too far out of reach
But with the memories we have
And pass down
From one to another
It's impossible to forget those
Who are no longer with us.

For Tracey Sanders, Jemma Sanders and Jodie Sanders

Tracey, may those memories never fade
And I hope you and your daughters make, create and build new
    ones
Jodie, sadly you never got to meet your granddad
But ask your mum if he would be proud of you
He is, and Tracey, you can see it every time you look in the mirror
And at your daughters.

Dad's Promise

A man sits with his head in his hands as his world comes to a bleak end. The rain shows no sympathy as it drowns him in the openness of his deserted soul. In his desperation he chooses to take his own life; an act that takes great conviction and lowness of the highest degree. He now lays and waits for the weakness to drain from his wrists, when voices speak to him "Why have you come here before your time? You shouldn't have, and those that do, come of their own free will, but lose it when they enter here."

The now dying man says, "I had it all, work that had me creating and making crystal worlds that people would see through, in an array of colours. I gave years of love to a woman who cast it aside for another, and I have no strength to go on. So it has me now on the doorstep of death."

The voices separated into three individual beings.

"I just want to die," he said, "Let me be, and do what you want with my body when I am sound asleep."

The three said "We will keep you company so that you don't travel alone."

Two of them each held his hand, while the other laid his head on his lap.

"Isn't there anything that would heal these untimely wounds?"

"There is," he said, "But today I lost the strength to go on and it's too late to undo what's been done."

With that they kissed his wrists and the deep crevices closed with no scars.

"We don't want you here and you must go, you have much to guard and raise."

And so he did, his skin shone, he grew warm again and his heart
was renewed like a new day at midnight.
The years trickle by, and to this day he continues to grow strong.
Thanks to the memory of a promise he made long ago to the
three voices of Caitlin, Samuel and Louise, who saved him; he
wouldn't give up living for them, because they hadn't given up
on him.

A man has many strengths
But are they found in his sturdy handshake?
Or the strain in his arms as he holds many loads?
It's found in many forms
But none more so than in the strength
That his children give him.

For Caitlin, Samuel and Louise Brook
From a father
Rob Brook, whose strength
And love is unbreakable
A love that every child should have.

Tender Years

There was a young child that sat in a room, frightened and tearful, looking for someone to comfort her and free her world from sadness. She longs to be held, but such acts of love are not gifted to her. In another room like this there is another child that stands in a cot crying, waiting for hands to pluck him from his wooden cell. The little girl makes her way to his bedroom and reaches in through the bars, into his world.

"There, there, don't cry I will keep you company," she says, "As that's what brothers and sisters do."

His crying eases and his tiny fingers reach out to touch his sister's nose. She giggles with joy and smiles in awe, "One day brother, we will be far away from here and this will be like a nightmare that we woke from."

Suddenly, the door bursts open and cruel hands descend down from the heavens like crows on a corpse. She is dragged kicking and screaming, like the wailing ocean currents.

"I told you, don't ever leave your room! Ever! You hear me?"

Shaking and weeping, she is restrained like a wild animal, and burnt with a hot pot of coffee, scarring her arm for life.

"Please Mummy, please it hurts! Please stop!" she screams.

"You want to leave do you? Who would ever want a stain like you in their life?"

These are the cruel words of a mother, who has two gifts, that she cares not for her children, and has acts of wickedness that would break even the most hardened of hearts.

That night the little girl makes a bid for freedom, and sneaks into
  her brother's room and wakes him, "Shhhhh don't cry I will
  come back for you, I promise."
She kisses his small soft hand, sneaks out of the house and makes
  off down the street.
The child now stands lost and lonely with her hands at her sides.
  Her bottom lip starts to quake as her eyes well up and
  overflow.
A door opens and a warm light shines over her as hands reach
  down and lift her skywards, "How did you get here little one?"
  said a voice that knew of compassion.
She told him of her story that broke his heart and made him
  happy that he could save her.
"I will save you and your brother," he said, "For to shy away and
  turn a blind eye is as evil as the deed that your own flesh and
  blood has strewn upon your body. When you move through
  life and have children of your own, you will shower then with
  love like this world has never seen."
Years pass and the girl grows and blooms into a beautiful young
  woman. Her brother grows too, freed from those wooden bars
  that held him lonely.
She now has kids of her own and as she passes a window, she sees
  the scar that her mother gave her; the only gift she was given,
  so painful and sad.
She wonders whatever happened to her, and if she went on to
  have more children.
She touches the scar that still lingers and says to herself, "I
  learned more from the healing wounds of my mind, body and
  heart than I ever learned from or was taught by my mother."
She smiles, looks to the sky and walks on into life's horizon.

The love we are meant to receive
Should be pure, warm and unconditional
From those that give us life,

Not abuse, neglect and utter abandonment.
How many children go through this on a day to day basis?
I can't think or say, and that saddens me
And for each one saved I shed a quiet tear.

For Anouska Young
You found your freedom and saved your brother
And may the life you live now
Be as happy as the thousands of tears, smiles and kisses that this
life can give.

The Verses Of Some

I've written many stories
That came from
Within
Created so many visions
I don't know
Where to begin
I've written of love
That took away my breath,
It was unbreakable, undiminished
Even in death,
I spoke of a man that could heal your wounds,
Who was cursed with a gift
If only you knew
For the gift he had
Was indeed so great,
He gave it away and sealed
Another's dark fate
I told you of a mother who found
Children in the park,
She knew of their essence
Within her own heart
It was her children from so long ago,
Her daughter so pale
Like the winters warm snow
I've written of pain
and of broken hearts,
Versed of a lady who was

Gifted with art
I wrote for Emma, Chris and Tricia Dean,
You told me your lives
And it has touched me
There's a place that's strange
A path I once took,
With a white and blue screen
And they called it Facebook
It's here I met
So many kind faces,
So many tortured souls
That had been in dark places
For Cat , Julie, Rob and dear Mike,
May our friendships continue
And may we
Never lose sight
For friends come and go
Like The Verse for the Departed,
With out Facebook
Our friendships would not
Have started
But we've all found each other
It's strange don't you think,
For we all have a passion
For scales and ink
I was given an idea
And ever since I've been hooked,
To write of our lives
And engrave in a book ,
Its not a best seller
It won't make a movie ,
It's my legacy I leave
For those that knew me
I wrote these stories

In the dark and completely nude,
I told you of my
Struggle "My Departure of Solitude"
For that is the title
Of my book yet to be born,
Twisted chapters
Of lessons in life healed and torn
I spoke of a dark friend
Who's always with me,
I said I'd give him all my money
If he'd just let be
Do you remember I cried "You're no friend of mine"
We fought
In the darkness
In that dungeon of my dark mind
I said we battled and raged
For many to see,
I do believe I wrote "This Dark Friend will never leave
    me"
But he found my stories
And he started to read,
I sat with delight as his eyes
Started to bleed,
He begged for forgiveness
All I gave him was laughter,
For now the tide had turned
I was his master
I said "Keep the book and read the stories,
They're the lives of people
Their hopes loves and glories"
For Cathy's and Mhairi's story
Will warm your black heart,
You have no friends
Except the lonesome cold dark

I've forgotten a few names
There's many to mention,
But you'll all be in the book
And that's my intention
Now pull up a chair take a seat at my side,
I have something to say
Before we say our goodbyes
Just listen once more
That's a great start,
I'm no writer, not gifted
for that's a fine art,
I've just written a few lines
May be a chapter or two,
I wrote a book in a room
Without a view,
But this is it
You can make up your minds,
I will always say
Your words are truly kind
Now Its getting late
Place this book on your shelf
And I thank you all greatly
I'm not talented
I was just being myself.

Thief Of Hearts

He sat in plain view with many others that claim to be like him, a great thief. They were all draped in fine clothes and wore many precious rings, stones and pearls about their person. A man, whose hands sparkled like the stars with many great rings called out to him, "Who are you? For we do not know you and we are like family here."

He looks up and replies, "Good evening Sir, that is true, we have not met before, nor do I know any of you. But do remember there is no honour among thieves."

Having addressed all in the tavern, he returns to his distant gaze.

The man, now angry at his question unanswered, calls for silence in the tavern. "I said, what is your name? For it looks as though you've only ever stolen the rags that you're wearing off a corpse!"

As the tavern roars with laughter, the man's eyes slice from left to right, looking at all the souls lost in their greed

"You wish to know my name, but what use is a name when you take from those that don't see the deeds that you do to them, those that are weaker and in need? You don't ask them their names."

"Wise words from a penniless, broke tramp," said the jewelled man.

"My name is …"

A silence fell like death in a graveyard that is untouched by life.

A man shouts, "You're a great thief of all sorts and your name is legendary amongst us, but you look as though you have fallen foul to another, who has taken your great wealth."

He looked and said, "I have lifted many great items in my time young man, I wore the crown of a king that I took while he slept, slipped many rings from unknowing hands and even precious stones from around many fair maidens' necks. But I can steal something more wondrous than what glitters and sparkles."

The jewelled man hissed, "If you are who you say you are, prove it!!! Why are you dressed like a beggar and what could be richer than a king's treasure chest?"

The man stood and emptied his pockets and all he had was a few coins.

"That's all I have and there is no need for me to prove who I am, or what I am able to do; for yes, I am a great thief, some may say legendary, but it's easy to take from those that have so little. I only took from those that had too much."

With that he put his coins back into his pocket.

"But where is all your wealth man???"

He said, "You ask me what is richer than a king's treasure chest to steal? That Sir, is easy! A woman's heart, for it's worth more than a mountain of gold, a river of diamonds and a tree laden in silver."

Many men nodded in agreement with him.

"You ask me where my wealth is, and it is true I have fallen foul of a thief greater than me."

"That's impossible, you're the greatest!" shouts a man.

"I gave away my mountain of gold, drained the river of all its diamonds and chopped down the tree of silver. All for the touch a woman's lips. And with the wealth I gave her she is now a queen in a distant land."

At this, the men clap and cheer his name, like the kings of old. He slips his hood up and shakes the jewelled man's hands.

"You have given us an amazing tale, is there anything you need? Some coins to see you on your way?"

I smiled and said, "You're too kind. But I have all I need, thank you anyway."

As I walked away the man shouted, "So how is it she is a greater thief than you?"

And I looked into the palm of my hand at the ring I have slipped from him and think, "No honour among thieves."

And I grin. Standing there in the doorway watching the rain beat down on the dark road ahead I turn and say, "Don't you know? She stole my heart."

Words Of A Boy

A king sat upon a throne and before him stood three assassins
accused of trying to murder him.

The first was a man built like a mountain, hands as big as lion's
paws and as strong as a bear.

The king asked, "How were you going to kill me?"

The man replied, "With my bare hands, for I can crush a man's
skull with ease."

The king said, "Hang the man."

And so it was done.

The second man was not like the one before; he was tall and slim
and bore a grim expression.

The king asked, "And what of you, how were you going to kill
me?"

The man said, "I am faster than a cheetah and would have slit
your throat as quick as lightning!"

The king replied, "Not fast enough though."

And he too was hung.

Now stood before him was a young boy, the king laughed, "A boy
wanting to do a man's work; how old are you boy?"

"I am seven years old my Lord."

The king laughed again. "How were you going to kill me?" he
bellowed.

"I am still going to kill you my Lord," replied the boy.

"But how?" he chuckled.

The boy said before the court, "I am not as strong as a bear; I have
not the strength to wield a sword, for I am but a child. I am

not as fast as lightning and cannot hide a dagger in these threads I wear."

The king looked on and asked, "Then how???"

The boy looked up from his small world and said, "I will kill you with words."

The king laughed, "Words are weak, steel is stronger."

The boy said "Come closer my lord, I want to whisper in your ear."

The king leaned over and the boy drew near and whispered for only the king to hear. He whispered words that even I dare not repeat.

The king said, "Let him go, he is but a worm and of no threat."

The boy was banished from the kingdom, but that night the king awoke screaming and crying, for the voices that tormented him drove him mad. In his blind rage and madness the king hung himself from a window overlooking his empire. The boy had indeed killed the king. For steel rusts and wanes but words are more powerful than an army of knights.

Nobody knows what happened to the boy. Some say he died alone, others say he never left the castle and is still there hiding in the shadows.

But now you are reading this and wondering, "How do I know what he said to the king and the words I shall not repeat????"

Because the boy, who looked weak and had just words to arm himself with, was me…

The Wishing Well

He stands looking up
At a faraway sky,
Listening to the echoes
As the birds
Pass by
In a place that the sun barely sees,
While catching the scent
Of the autumn leaves
There in the hole of a dark abyss,
He looked in the
Shadows
For a woman that he missed
Someone so strange
So dark and rare,
The colours of flames
Etched in her hair
The scratching and clawing
On the
Cold heartless stones,
Imprisoned in a place he crafted
From his dark soul
Screaming and shouting 'til he
Loses his voice,
Battling the walls that
Gave him no choice
There in the silence and the dead
Of the night,
He found many coins that

Had been lost in sight
Revealed by the moon on a
Pale Winter's eve,
He could bribe the shadows
In order to leave
But this place, that's
Spiteful and cruel,
Many made their wishes here
That never came true
He collected the coins one by one,
Until they were stacked
So high
And he could see the sun
He began to climb
And left the ground,
Strength restored
He was no longer bound
Reaching up
Clinging onto hope,
As his hands stretched out
And reached a forgotten
Lost rope
Reaching the top he gave a cry,
He said to himself
"I'm alive, I did not die"
There in his pocket
A coin was in place,
He looked around and now
Knew of this place
He kissed the coin
That fell deeper than Hell,
And wished for that woman
For this
Was a wishing well.

Companions

How do you measure a friendship? Is there a way to test its
strength? Is it possible that such a bond can be found?
I knew a man who had found that amazing connection, a
friendship that ran deeper than any ocean. This is his story.
All his life this young man struggled to make friends, he was
considered by many as a loner, a hobo if you will. Never
knowing who to trust, who to talk to and if love would ever
enter his gloomy world.
One day while by himself on the outskirts of the city he met a
stranger who was also by himself. He spoke to the stranger
who now stood in his path.
"Hello, what's your name and are you like me?"
The lost soul stood, staring at him, eyes fixed and alert but never
spoke.
"It's ok, you don't have to tell me right now, just be nice if you
would stay and keep me company, and I the same for you."
The stranger's eyes said it all. It's a moment that very few will ever
have, and from that moment on they never left each others'
side.
At night they'd huddle together to keep warm, share food and
expressed emotions and kindness that many laughed at, but
they didn't care. For they had something unique and truly
breathtaking to see.
As time drew on they grew old and grey together. One night in a
poorly lit alleyway the two companions were making their way
through the dark. A man stepped from the shadows and pulled
a gun. "Empty your pockets or I will shoot your worthless
friend!"

The young man said in a hurry, "Oh please, don't shoot my
friend! He is harmless and never speaks. Take my money, my
watch and my coat."

The man takes all he can and walks away laughing at his shameless
deed but he stops and out of pure malice, he raises his arm and
opens fire. His silent friend leaps in front of his companion
and takes the bullets that send him crashing to the floor, but
even then he limps to his feet, defends his friend and attacks
the man, but again he is cut down by bullets.

He lays there motionless and his friend lays him in his lap.
Cradling him he cries "Please boy, don't go you're all I have
and love, it should have been me, not you."

The tears slice down his face and splash soundlessly onto his
companions face. Still his friend says nothing but again his
eyes say it all, like they did many years ago. With that his
companion, his soul mate drifts silently away, so far and out of
reach.

I never had a friend like that again and I doubt I ever will. You
only ever make the connection like that once in your life. So
you see, that's how it works with 'One man and his dog.'

Yes, now the penny drops, a man and his companion,

A friendship that requires no words, just trust and love.

So, if you have such an amazing bond with a companion in your
life

Cherish them, as they would lay down their life for you.

And I hope you would do the same for them.

Paintings

I knew a woman who was blessed with a magical gift; she could
paint anything your heart desired. Such was her gift that many
came from far and wide to have their own masterpiece created.
She said, "All the time you come here and never ask me to paint
for you."
"Your gift is amazing, but I could not afford to buy or pay for such
works of art."
She put down her brush and drew closer to me.
"What is it that your heart desires? " I said "You can't paint what I
lost, it's not possible and it's torture for my heart."
She touched my face and whispered, "Tell me please, as I sense
you have lost someone close to you."
My eyes filled with tears, they slipped silently down my cheeks
and my lips trembled, "My son."
"Your son, where is he?" she said.
I fought back the tears but the waves were too strong. I said, "My
son was my world,
just a boy when he slipped away into a sleep where there are no
dreams. I am hollow without hearing his laughter."
She held me for what must have been only a moment but felt like
a lifetime.
"I will paint your son for you; tell me, what did he look like?"
So I told her and she began to paint with such grace and passion,
that an astounding amount of hours passed as the night
lingered with us.
"There, almost finished, take a look," she said.
It was amazing, my son looked so real; I could have held his hand.

"I am speechless at what you have created, if only it was real."

She said, "Paintings are like memories it's that special moment captured for all of time."

"I can't afford to buy it," I said.

"It's not for sale my love."

At that, my shoulders dropped and my head sank lower than my heart could beat.

"But the painting is not finished, it's missing something."

"What?" I replied.

She smiled, "You of course."

I grew sad and worthless. "What for? I can't buy it anyway. Looking at it would drive me to the brink of sadness."

She said, "Look at the painting and see."

So I did, and as I looked on, the painting moved, the birds in the background were flying and the trees swayed in the breeze.

Then I saw my son reach out from the painting, "Daddy, take my hand, it will be like it was and we will never be parted again."

His hand touched mine and the hollow empty void was filled with his laughter once more.

"Thank you, I don't know to thank you!"

She placed her hand on my shoulder, "Your son is waiting and you have waited long enough."

With that I stepped from this world into another with my son, we walked into the sunset that she had painted and I knew that the brush strokes had brought me to life again.

So next time you see such a work of art,

Maybe, just maybe, you will think and wonder

"What if?"

And I leave you with that warming thought.

Captain Carnage Origins

He was left in a dumpster for dead in an alleyway filled with many
shadows. No name, no clothes, not even a kiss goodbye. Just a
blanket as he was left to his fate in the filth and stench.

An old man and lady are putting away the rubbish from their shop
which had built up from the days work. As they go to drop the
rubbish bags in, the lady hears the cries and sobbing. "Oh my
Lord, look!"

As they peer in, they see a small boy amongst the newspapers and
grime.

"We can't leave him," she said and lifted him from certain death.

"What are we going to do with him?" said her husband.

"Well, nobody wanted him."

He took his cap and shook his head in disbelief, "You can't be
serious! At our age, what we going to tell people?" yet she
cradled him as her own.

"Are you listening to me woman? We can't!"

But it's too late; she ignores him and goes inside, out of the gloom
of the alleyway.

"We'll say he's our granddaughter's child come to stay."

The husband replies, "What??? We don't have any kids, we can't
just pick a child off the street and say, there you go, he's ours!"

They argue into the night but in the end he understands that
every child needs a home and not a bin for a resting place.

He is brought up above the shop, cared for and loved as their
own. The shop is popular with many kids of all ages, buying
this and that for a few cheap laughs. For this long lost lad who
was saved lives above a joke shop where much fun is to be had

on every shelf. Bangers, invisible ink pens and fake sick sit in
neat piles. Party outfits and dress up costumes are also sold
here, but the boy's main love is for crazy super glue; he's
always gluing things down at school, spraying fart spray in the
girls' toilets and shit in a can that gets squirted in the teachers'
drawers. The teachers think he's chaos but the kids love him.
"Sent home from school again, what you done this time?"
"Mum it isn't me this time, honest," he says with a smile that's
    hard to hide.
"Come on; tell me what you did or no TV and no pudding."
And he rolls his eyes, "Ok, ok, you know Dad ordered that itching
    powder?"
"Hmmmmm, I told him not to," she said in a sharp voice.
"Well I emptied it."
She raised one eyebrow, "YOU EMPTIED IT WHERE????"
Looking up, he pulls a stupid 'I don't know look' on his face.
"Er, I emptied it into the sports teacher's jock strap when I snuck
    into the changing rooms."
She blows her top,"Yoooooou little shhhi…"
But then snorts of laughter from behind the door comes falling
    out; "Hahahahah son you did it then!"
She turns, "I might have bloody known you had a hand in this!"
"Me? Come on, just having a laugh the boy was. Right son?"
And the boy is laughing as loud as his dad.
"Dad, you should have seen him, he was mad as hell, all the kids
    loved it, and seeing them smile was worth the clip round the ear."
At that his dad scruffs up his hair, "That's my boy, always making
    people smile and setting them at ease."
His wife cross, says, "Right, the pair of you can sweep up, and as
    for you, young man, no pudding, And you, old man, should
    know better!"
As the two clowns continue giggling, they sweep up and cash up
    the till, then the door opens and the bell rings as a young girl
    steps in.

"Er, we are closed young miss."

She replies, "That's ok I just wanted to say that was a great prank you did at school."

The boy turns and replies, "I just like seeing people smile and I am happy to entertain you all."

"Well you do a good job; don't think the teachers see it that way though. Hahahaha well, just wanted to say, you keep us smiling."

As she leaves she turns and says, "The teachers call you a trouble maker, but you're not."

"Well what would you call me then?"

She looks up thinking and says, "I don't know, I'd call you… Captain Carnage,"

she laughs, "See you at school."

He thinks, "Hmmmmmm Captain Carnage, what do you think Dad?"

"Son, whatever makes you smile."

As they leave a shelf breaks and the items fall on top of the boy and a wig falls on his head along with a box of masks that spill out over the floor.

"Leave it son, we'll tidy up tomorrow. Let's go upstairs and have dinner."

They do, but just beforehand, he picks up a mask and puts it on. Looking in the mirror, wearing the mask and wig he whispers to himself "Captain Carnage" and runs upstairs.

From that moment on, a strange being is born.

To be continued…

Freedom

I met an old man on death row many years ago. He had spent half his life locked in a cell. I said, "Tell me sir, what is your crime that has put you here?"

He said, "I wanted to be a free man; free from rules, free to speak my mind at the injustice I see and speak words that give others hope. This they fear."

"How long have you been here in this darkened place?" I asked.

He said, "Thirty years my dear boy and my wife died of a broken heart many years ago."

I looked at the old man and wept for his freedom. How I longed to set him free. The worn man asked, "Why do you cry for a stranger that you barely know?"

I said, "You have given up your freedom; I am saddened that you cannot walk in long grass or sit under a tree and feel the rain upon your skin."

The man said, "I am a free man."

"But how?" I asked.

He said, "In my mind I can transcend time and space, I break down these walls and walk amongst the winds that ripple the waters edge. In my mind I burst into life and wipe the tears from the eyes of those who need hope and love. These walls cannot hold me."

He placed his hand on my head and said to me a warming voice, "All men are free if they want to be. Tell me son, who is more free, a man who lives a life in fear and doubt and never says what he feels? Or a man who speaks in such a way that it frightens even the gods? I am a free man and this I will prove to you."

The next day at sunset the man was taken to a hill and a noose
placed around his neck. He looked over at me, smiled and
said, "I am free in my heart, mind, body and soul. I am free
now but you, young man, must hang me."

"I can't," I said, "I cannot end your life."

I stepped back and refused to kill the man.

"Then you too will join him!"

We both now stood with nooses around our necks. The old man
held my hand and said, "Don't be afraid, you are free and a
free man has no fear in his heart."

And with that, we broke down the walls and walked in the long
green grass once more.

Wanting To Smile

Ever wonder why that person
Is so funny?
How it is they can summon
Laughter at will?
Make a thousand people smile
And leave you wanting more?
Did you ever stop to think
That maybe, just maybe
They would like
To smile too and laugh as you do?
Don't be fooled by his jokes
The misdirection and his
Sleight of hand
For these are all just smoke screens
That hide
A fateful truth;
Maybe one day he will smile
And laugh and be like you.

Seize The Day

I had this one moment,
I took just one
Glance,
At something so real
Not a half mistaken chance
It was there
And I felt so sure,
For it made the sound of waves
Breaking
Against the rocky shore
I did not seek it,
I wish I gave chase,
But it slipped through my fingers
Such a painful, lost waste
I looked on
And I clawed in hope,
But all I could feel was the tightening
Of the rope
I took too long, and lost my way
I'd forgotten my promises
And she faded away
I pounded my fists
Against the cold naked floor
Longing to touch you
I wish I had done more
I crawled and rolled on
My knees and hands
But that magical chance was swallowed

And lost in quicksand
I staggered and swayed lost in a breeze,
But in the end
I guess it just wasn't meant to be
I'll never forget the sunset
As it shone in her face,
But she was a mystery, impossible
To replace
I sit and wonder
At what might have been,
A lost opportunity, an amazing sight very seldom seen.
I'll recall all we said
All the smiles and laughter,
Fragments of beauty
Will remain hereafter
If you have that moment
And you catch her gaze,
Let her see you smile and start a blaze
For those moments
Come few and far between,
Don't make the mistake
Don't follow me
So take that chance and
Don't turn away,
Grab her tight
Hold your breath
"And seize the day".

Sarah

I met a child in my dreams. She was a world of wonder and
perfection. Her skin was as soft as snow but warm as the earth.
I said, "Dear girl, why do you come to me in my dreams?"
Her voice was light and gentle and the sound of innocence.
"I am your dream and I am here to keep you safe. I give you hope
when all you know is despair. When your world is empty and
you long for me, you will remember my name and that's
when I come to you. When you need me most."
I bent down on one knee and said, "But why in dreams, for I wish
to have you for all time. I know when I wake you will have
gone again; this is torment for my mind and the crippled heart
that barely beats in my chest."
The little girl placed both hands on my face and held it like the
universe holds the stars. "Don't cry, please be one and whole.
For you long for a gift that is wasted by many and held dear by
so few. Some never know what they have and others would
trade their shadow just to hold me in their arms."
"What I long for is you dear child, I wish to see you run and hold
you high to the heavens, so that the world knows that I am
you, and you are me."
The little girl whispered, "There is always hope; never forget that
without hope, where would the heart be? Would it beat? For
without hope, prayer, emotion and kisses we would all only be
lost in dreams. You are tired;" she said, "Close you eyes and
rest and when you wake you will remember all I have said."
My eyes felt heavy and I started to drift. "Before I fall asleep tell
me your name."
"You know my name and I know yours; you are my mother and I
am your Sarah."

Coming Back

Please forgive me for my
Absence of late,
For I have missed you all
And you left
Open the gate
I went to a place on the far
Edge of time,
To a place I created in
My own mind
There in my solace and the
Confines of my rapture,
I lost that spark
The magic you loved
That I longed to recapture
I sought the answers
On a cosmic tide,
Looking for clues that the world
Tried to hide
I was given a glimpse at what
Was, and what
Should have been,
But there in a haze of smoke
I should have seen
It was to cloud my judgment and my dark choices,
But I have silenced
The cruel tongue of those
Empty voices
Now my skin burns
And the sweat

Drips from my face,
The fire reignited in my fingertips,
I will engulf this place
So do forgive me
For my absence of late,
I am the owner, defender
Of Hells Gate
I was a pupil and I became
Grand teacher,
Smile my loves
For the return of Hells Preacher.

The Unnamed

A young man was asked by a group of people, who were sat drinking
and laughing by a camp fire under a blanket of night stars, if he
had ever been in love, or touched a girl and made her ache.

He sat and wondered what to say to such a question, when one
man shouted, "Come on, we're waiting boy, have you? Or do
you not know of life's pleasures?"

He looked at him and his friends. And he glared at the flames that
lit up all their eyes in the coldness of the dark.

"Does it matter if I tell you, for as long as I know, that's all that
matters?"

The man sat there and bellowed, "You are just a boy, yet to be a
man, and I doubt that any women would flock to your bed."

"My thoughts and heart are my own and I choose not to say that
which would make you envy me."

He climbs to his feet and pulls a blade that shimmers in the fire's
glow. "If you don't tell me, I'm going to steal your vision from
you."

The young man smiled and looked around him. "Why are you
bothered so much by what I have seen or might have had? For
have you not lived a life of wine and women?"

And with that the young man is set upon like helpless prey before
a pack of wolves. He's kicked and beaten until his face lies in a
puddle of his tears and blood.

"Going to tell us now boy?" sneered the tyrant.

He looks up but takes a kick to the face that splits it in two. "Why
do you beat me so? What gain and pleasure do you get?" he
said as he struggled to talk through split lips.

To that, the man replied, "I heard that you had a lady friend a long time ago, said to be a rare find."

The young man nodded, "I did but I don't care what you do, for she is too unique for words."

So they hold him down and place his hands into the fire. Screams slice the air and not even the night dared move.

"Tell me boy, for if you don't, I will kill you and burn your body."

The young man sat there rocking and cradling himself in pain.

"Are you sure you want to know?" he said with a grin.

And they all cheered. "Tell us boy, we need a laugh."

And he said, "Then so be it."

They huddle in close as the young man tries his best to nurse his wounds.

"I did meet a woman once. It was at the crossroads on a night like this, but darker and the chill in the air was deathly still."

As he spoke a dark cloud fell upon them.

"She was amazing, a beauty like no other of this world. She possessed such a body that even the gods admired her. When she spoke she could steal men's hearts in a moment and lay waste to their souls in the blink of an eye. To hold her in your arms is to embrace the very hottest flames in Hell. But to take a kiss from her lips will tear you in two and heal you as quick as the sun melting the snow in the spring."

The men's mouths hung open and they were stunned into silence.

"You asked me and I have told you, have I not?" he said.

The tyrant said, "You expect us to believe you? Hahaha" he chuckled.

"I do, for she was, and still is, my greatest love ever, and held longer than you've held any woman."

The tyrant sat there and asked, "What was her name then, she must have had a name?"

He sat there and smiled, and then raised one eyebrow. "You really want to know her name?" he said.

"Yes we do, come on, tell us."

And so, he whispered it into one of the men's ears.

"Now whisper to the next man and so forth."

He did, and one by one they grew afraid and begged for forgiveness. "Sorry we didn't know. Please have mercy on us!"

With that, one by one they leapt into the flames, thinking it would save them. He did indeed meet a woman at the crossroads.

The woman he met was amazing, stunning like the night sky, beautiful as the Earth and wondrous as the Abyss of Souls. For when you have lost your mind, heart and soul to the Angel of Hell, getting beaten and burnt is a mere raindrop in a puddle.

For to survive a night's passion with her is unheard of.

Oh, and how do I know of this story?

Well, I know her name. Wondering what it is?

I can't tell you that. I fell in love with her. And sold my soul to her and her forked tongue.

Ink

I sat with a stranger who barely
Moved his hands,
As he laid down the ink on my body
I am blank page man
As he took his time painting my skin,
I told him tales of Darkness
And sin
He said "Tell me young man, why do you
Wish for such stains",
So I sang him a song of a life
Filled with pain
I sang of times when
I wanted the end,
As he leaned over closer, his back
Starts to bend
I sat and listened as the steel stratched my surface,
Creating from his mind with a Hell
Bent purpose
A design I suggested from my
Dark soul,
But this will take many hours
Before he reached his goal
He explained and said
"Many don't understand,
For I was taught and guided by
An ancient man
The man who taught me

Could instil such vision,
He could lay down a master piece
With perfect precision
But like all paintings and souls
That are jaded,
He passed away long ago
But his ink
Never faded"
The artist said
"I am finished please take a
Closer look,
At these verse's I inked on your skin
Like a forgotten lost book"
And indeed he was right and his
Skill was great,
For no one could Argue
Nor debate
That we who wear our ink
In the
Light and dark,
We appreciate such greatness
For this is not
Poor mans art.

Escape

I have seen many lands
Barren and bare,
Swam in oceans without a care
I've walked many miles
All alone,
Found myself distant
And far from home
I've crossed many rivers
Stood naked in lakes,
There's no chains that can
Hold me, no chains
I can't break
I sat and watched the sunrise
In faraway places,
Met so many people
And so many different races
This road that I walked
I travelled alone,
Maybe someday I'll find someone to call
My own
So join me if you will
And walk the path
That I take,
We're roaming
Free now
It's time to escape

Inspired

In a time long ago, there was a man who was given the gift of
storytelling. He had written many strange and wonderful tales.
Some loved to read his stories believing they were real and
true, and they gave others hope and ideas.

But in this kingdom books and such storytelling are outlawed.
News had reached the king that this storyteller had come to
town and now lived nearby. The king was not amused and
sent his knights to get him. They found him living in a room
in a dark, dirty alleyway where the smell was coarse and foul.
They broke down the door and stepped in and down into a
dark room lit only by candles.

"We have been sent by our king; he has summoned you to his…"

And the man holds out his hand and gestures to the knight to stop
talking, "Your king has summoned me you say? I do not parley
with such fools."

So they seize him and then start to beat him until he can resist no
longer. He is stripped and dragged through the streets for the
world to gaze upon. He stumbles and falls headfirst into a
dirty puddle that washes his blood soaked face. He is kicked
and punched as one man urinates on him, stinging his open
wounds. He's chained to a horse that now drags him through
the streets and to the palace.

As they step before the king in his great hall, he is thrown to the
cold marble floor, whimpering in pain.

"My Lord here he is," said the knight, as the man lay in his own
blood and saliva.

"So you are the one corrupting my peoples minds? Well, speak up man!" shouted the king as his voice echoed in the great hall.

The man looked up from his bloodied world and said, "What right do you have to treat another human being like this? What great power was bestowed upon you from on high like a god?" He spat blood on the floor in defiance.

"Gods man!!!!!! I am a god, I choose who's free and who's a prisoner; I decide who eats and starves and it is me who decides who lives and who dies!" said the king. He addresses the court and sends word, "Anybody who reads his books will be put to death."

The man heaves himself up onto all fours, gathering breath and with what strength he has left, stands wavering from side to side. "Why are you so afraid of me and my stories? Like a king about to lose his worth to an overwhelming army?"

The king in a rage barked, "What did you say? Afraid??? I'm afraid of you???"

Then draws his sword and impales the man in his torso, thrusting it deep and everlasting into him. He staggers back and falls to the floor. The king raises his blade for the final act when a tiny figure cries out, rushes forward and shields the now dying man.

"What are you doing boy? Know your place!" said the king.

But the boy refuses to move.

"No matter, he is all but dead anyway," said the king as He walked back to his throne. The man lay dying, his blood flooding out onto the cold stone floor. The boy held his hand and said, "Your stories are amazing; you give hope to those that need it and adventures to those that are too afraid to seek them. I have read your stories and they have shaped my young life."

The storyteller looked at him with a dying glow in his eyes and said, "I am glad you like my stories, but it seems that my part in this story called life is at an end."

His grip on the boys hand softens, his face eases and like the front cover of an old book, he fades away.

The boy kisses his hand and his face, then glides his fingertips down and closes the storyteller's eyes. As the body of the storyteller is dragged away, I can't help but feel that a part of me has died writing this story.

"Father, you said all those that read his tales must die, that means me too then, as I have and will continue to read his stories, for they are greater than any deeds you have ever done," said the son of the king

"You want to read, do you boy, my Son the Traitor? I won't kill you, for that is too kind, no, you will be banished, never to return!"

The boy wept at this act, but also looked at the pool of innocent blood on the floor left by the storyteller.

"Before I go father, I ask for three gifts to send me on my way."

His request is met; he is given ink, a quill pen to write with and a book filled with blank paper to write of his own adventures and all that life can show him.

I miss that storyteller from old, but in his final moments he taught that boy more than any book could ever teach him.

He taught me whether you write one story or a thousand books, if you can touch just one soul in the world with your words your life is amazing and complete.

Wards

What do you do when all hope is lost? And all the words you can
  muster won't ease that blackness that washes over you, and
  you long for answers that elude you?
I sat with a young boy the other day, not an old man who was wise, or
  a fortune teller who claims great visions, but a boy barely into his
  teens. We sat gazing through a window looking out onto the
  outside world. His skin was pale but he had a smile of a thousand
  colours, eyes that were young but full of many memories.
I said to him, "It's a lovely day isn't it?"
And he replied in a soft voice, "You lie, for it is a beautiful day, far
  richer than lovely, don't you think?"
And I had to agree it was.
"Tell me," he said, "What's your life been like? Has it been
  everything you've wanted and expected?"
I turned and smiled and said, "You ask great questions that are
  deep and meaningful, you have the face of a child who hasn't
  seen enough sunsets and stars, and yet you have a way about
  you, that's of great wisdom of thought."
He tilted his head towards me and said, "So has it been what you
  expected then?"
"Yes it has, it's had moments of tears and laughter, and I have seen
  amazing sights and saved many people. But I have also lost
  many to this terrible battle and when that happens, a part of
  me dies, I am told I shouldn't feel that."
He then did something amazing. He took my hand and we walked
  outside and stood in the warm wind, listening to the sounds
  that few people stop to hear, or care to listen to.
"That's me, that is," he said pointing to a boy who is running

down the street to the shops, "The man over there laughing with the love of his life, without a care in the world, but for her. And the old man who struggles to cross the road and make it to safety. That's what I see when I'm sleeping."

I stand gently squeezing his hand; I look down at him and then place my hand on his naked head. "I am sorry that you won't be able to do or be any of these things. Today you have taught me so much, more than any book I have had to study."

He said, "I am tired now."

I take off my white coat and wrap him in it, pick him up and carry him to his room. I lay him down and cover him up with the sheets.

"How much pain are you in?" I asked.

And with courage he replies, "I was in pain but now it subsides, and I hurt almost no more."

I close the door, but I leave the curtains open to fill the room with the suns rays.

"I am sorry with all my heart and who I am that I could not save you."

I bite down to grit my teeth hard, and my throat tightens and grows coarse as I battle an army of tears and a legion of emotions.

"That's ok Doc, you did all you could, and I am grateful that you are here with me, you think you haven't saved me, but you have. For you have allowed me to dream a little longer than I expected and that is just as important as living."

And though I am told I am not meant to be moved by his words, I can't help but hold him one last time. I kiss his head and as his warm breath slows, he squeezes my hand one last time. I break in two as he falls softly to sleep for the last time.

I wish my words could heal the sick and relieve those that are in pain, to be able to give them just a little more time here with us, and I am sorry that they don't. But if words are all we have, then I beg you, don't hold them inside. For tomorrow may be too late, and how my heart falls, when the chance is lost forever…

Scars

Do you have scars?
I have scars.
These you can see, if you look closely.
But there are
Scars you can't see,
I won't let you.
For these are from battles and wars
Fought, lost and won
In my heart, mind, body and soul.
I will take your scars, heal you,
And make you new.
I have scars,
And I will share them with you.

The Night's Journey

Two friends and I sat late one evening, and with us sat a stranger whom we will all come to know when the time is right. The so-called stranger said, "Tell me, what have you done so far with your lives?"

So we sat and listened as one of my friends said "I haven't seen the world, I've never swam in waters in far off places and seen sunsets that would make me feel alive. I have yet to taste and feel the rain that falls on a summer's eve, and how I long for such simple pleasures."

I said, "I have done and seen those things and dreams that you so painfully want."

I looked to my other friend and said, "What do you pine for?"

He replied, "I have never walked naked in a shallow stream, and have the moon view me from the starlit sky. But what I long for, what I crave, more than life itself is a girl that holds my hand, allows me to weep and not think less of me. I would surrender all that I am to kiss her shoulders and hold her closer than the air that fills my body because without her I could not go on."

"That is more than most men will ever have, but may see from a distance."

"I have had those moments and like gravity, we were drawn to each other, and I did not squander a single moment. I have done and seen much, and I am complete."

Now the stranger said, "I have a long journey to take tonight, who'd like to keep me company?"

Both my friends argued who would go and who deserved it more.

The stranger said, "Please stop, for I have not told you where we will be going."

They both said, "We don't care, it's somewhere new and we need to go."

But I knew the stranger, for I was wiser than my friends.

I said, "I will go, and I am happy that my friends will stay; but I ask of you to live your lives as much as you can, and all that you crave for comes true."

My friends said, "That's unfair, you have done so much and we have not."

I smiled and said, "That's why I want to go, you have not lived as I have. You have not loved or been loved, and this gift I give to you both."

"What gift, where is it?"

The stranger put his arm around me and said, "It is time, the night long and road narrow."

We walked to the door and I turned and said to my friends, "The gift I give you, is life so make the most of this beautiful gift, for when it's gone it's gone forever."

Then it dawned on my friends, this was no stranger, or mere chance that he was here.

The door opened and I said, "Goodbye."

For my friend who now embraced me on the journey was indeed an angel; The Angel of Death.

Pebbles

I sat on a beach covered in stones,
Wasting my life away as the sun
Burnt my bones
I thought long and hard as to where my dream went,
The years washed away my life
It was all but spent.
I put on hold so many of my desires,
Helped so many others as my
Time expired
Many others' dreams came true,
But I was held back like a room
Without a view
I tried so hard to turn back the years,
But the emotions I felt left me
Drowning in tears.
I sat and cried and called to the winds,
As the storm continued
To rage within.
But amongst the stones and the
Broken glass,
Was a glimmer of hope that my
Time hadn't passed
For I found a stone that did not belong,
It wanted distant shores
It longed to be gone
So I looked to the sky and the waves
Ahead,

And my dreams returned for my
Heart bled,
For I knew I was different my father
Once said.
"Son you're not right, and you don't
Belong,
This life is not for you, you must
Be gone
Where you're going no one can say,
But I hope you make it and be
Happy some day"
My father was right he always knew,
That I'd leave this place
The room without a view
So with my dreams in my heart
And time on my side,
The day has now come to
Say goodbye I'll travel this earth but I'm
Not alone,
For I carry my friend that once
Lost lonely stone.

Blind Man Seeing

I met a blind man one day and asked him, "What's it like not to see?"

The man smiled and said, "I have been blind since birth, I know no different, I know not of the colour of the skies above or the shapes of clouds. I've never seen a sun set nor seen it rise. I haven't seen the ocean or a bird soar high into the heavens."

My heart sank and my head hung in sorrow.

The man reached out, touched me and said, "Lift your head and let your heart rise son, for it is true, I cannot see but I can hear the wind in the trees, feel the sun on my face and touch the ripples in the sea."

My heart grew and so did a smile on my young face.

He told me, "It's an amazing gift to be able to see the world, but if you don't stop to listen and touch it every now and then, who is more blind, me, an old man? Or you with your eyes wide shut? For to see is amazing, to feel is spellbinding."

Future's Remembered

A woman went down to the lake one night to die. There at the edge of the silvery glaze, with emotions she struggled to contain, she explored the surface for reasons why she should live or die.

She was met by a voice that skipped along the water like the reflections of the stars above. "Every night you come here asking the same question, asking dark matter to bear you henceforth to a cold wasteland."

She looked on, puzzled by the strange voice that reached out from the gloom.

"You don't know me, you don't know how I am suffering. You know not of my life and my tragedy," she said.

The voice continued, "Please tell me why you want to die and surrender this life for the next?"

The woman cried, put her fingers to her lips and then held herself for her own comfort. For it was plain to see what had happened.

"I had a little girl and she loved the lake. She was so fair and beautiful, but she drowned in the lake and I never found her body to lay her to rest. I want to feel nothing, and be nothing, as this guilt and life is my punishment now."

The voice now grew louder and caused the water to ripple. A figure came into view and stood upon the water as if it was solid rock.

"If you take my hand, I will ease your heart of your loss and make you numb. But to see your daughter again, this wish I cannot grant. For to take a life when so many want one is a crime that has no forgiveness, and you will see and feel much pity."

The woman pleaded with the figure that now stood over her. He placed his hands into the water and held the water like a newborn baby.

"Please look into the puddle," he said.

As she looked she saw a little girl playing and smiling, but she also saw a woman crying at the waters edge.

"I don't understand why you show me knowing it's torment, like a broken toy that is of no use."

He said, "Emily, please never stray too far, not even for a moment. For a moment can last a lifetime of sorrow and regret."

With that he let the water wash over her face, and as she opened her eyes, she was sitting still at the waters edge, wondering what had happened. She was cradled once more, this time by a mother's arms.

"You shouldn't play by yourself at the waters edge Emily," said the voice.

"I'm sorry mummy, I never will again."

We all glimpse the future at some point
And it's not always clear what we see
And what might be
But I am happy to sit here with you all
And see what the future holds.

Rooms

And if this room is my prison
And I can no longer leave,
Will you hold a gun
To my head
And so gently set me free
If I am bound and chained and
Left alone,
Will you let the rats in, let them
Gnaw me to the bone
When you have whipped
My body
And burned my skin,
Will you bend those bars
And let the rain wash in
For what you have done, the world
Will clearly see,
That I am innocent, it was you
Not me
You've stolen my heart and rotted
My mind,
Gave me empty rooms, treated
Me unkind
Gave me a hand to ease this pain,
Took my heart
Called me dark names
But take your time and have
Your fun,
For when I'm dead and your

Nightmare has begun
I will be there to claim my own
I'll see you in Hell
And reclaim my soul.

Magic Music

I sat with a gifted man in a room lit only by candles. We sat at a
piano that glistened in the rooms haze. His hands had seen
kinder times, for they were weary with time and age. He said,
"Music is more than just noise, it's more than a chaos of
sound that you sense in the air. Music is like life, it's about
hitting the right notes at the right time."
I asked, "Please show me, for my life so far has been out of tune
and of the lowest keys."
The old man said, "Tell me of your woes and your losses, as you
do, I will play and set your mind at ease."
I sat motionless.
"In your own time," he said.
I felt my throat tighten and my mouth became dry like a harsh
desert, but then I spoke,
"Many times I have been alone with just my shadow for company.
There were times when I felt so alive, so alive I could breathe
new life into a rose that's wilting at sunset."
He then played some notes and I felt so light.
"Continue," he said.
"There was a best friend and he said he'd never leave me, but he
went to a place where
there's no return."
Again his hands glided like water on ice, tapping out a melody that
was so personal to me.
"Continue," he said, "But only if you can."
"I had an angel once, with a smile that could light up a room and
warm your body like the sun in the spring, she had a body that

the gods envied, and so, in their selfish spite they cast her high into the stars and I lost her name."

The man stopped playing and said, "You have lost so much in such a short space of time my dear boy, I will play you a symphony that will shatter the sky and let her soul shower down around you, and you will be together again."

The music he crafted was beautiful, too beautiful for any words that could fall from my lips. I thanked the old man, left his room and stepped outside. The music grew distant, and it began to rain. I listened to the shower and I recalled her forgotten name…

The Dark Bar

She sat in the corner, almost out of sight in the smoky haze of a
back street tavern with just her thighs on show, displaying her
taught legs without a care for who stopped and lingered at her.
Many so-called men can be found here boasting of battles and
conquests of ladies' bodies. Men pass by hurling insults and
unsavoury gestures at her but she just looks through them like
glass with no reflection until something catches her eyes. A
figure draped and shrouded in mystery, all concealed but for a
rip that showed a strange mark on his leg. His face was held in
the folds of his hood as he served drinks to hordes of fools.
"Time gentlemen please," he called.
They spilled out into the alleyway that was spoilt with darkness.
He locked up and dimmed the lights further, as he did, he
removed his dressings and displayed himself before her, even
though he did not know she was there, still sitting in the
shadows. His skin was clean and smooth, with dark eyes that
glinted even in the poorest of light.
"Why do you hide such treasures from the world?"
He looked up and saw nothing, but knew he was not dreaming,
and then she stepped out from the dark.
"The bar is closed," he said.
"Indeed it is but you said gentlemen, not ladies, and I am far from
that."
He replied, "There is little money here to steal and I…"
He was stopped short as she removed her hood that had sheltered
her 'til now and unveiled her beauty; dark fiery eyes and deep
dark hair that stunned him and he was transfixed.

"Tell me what you want, for right now I am unable to fight you with a sword or my heart."

"I have watched you, the way you move, the way you speak and the manner in which you use your hands for working when they should be doing far more than this."

And so she glided over to him and, using both his hands, he cupped her supple peaks. In doing so, she slid one hand down into her aching gate, where she stroked her swollen spur in delight. She entered herself with soft moans of pleasure, placing her finger afterwards into his mouth where he sucked her life from her fingertips. Overcome, he tears her clothes from her body, the buttons falling, and becoming lost to the floor.

"Come here and linger at my fruits," she said. She sits open legged, teasing herself as her finger flays side to side over her spur, her lower back arches and her legs tremble as she reaches her verge. The man, now unable to hide his stern, unties his clothes from around himself, which hide his darkness and the strange shape on his leg. She licks her lips as he grasps himself, working his flesh that shines before her. She crawls like a shadow across the floor over to him, takes him in her mouth as cries of joy and wanting leave his lips. Running her tongue from the base of his foundation, she can feel the veins swell with every whip-like stroke that she delivers.

He looks down as she glares up at him like the Devil's whore and smiles as she thrashes her hands up'n'down his dark member.

Picking her up off the floor, he wraps her legs around his waist and impales her down into the deepest depths of her dungeon.

Quiet moans become louder and feverish as she cries out "Harder, come harder, fuck me faster until I break in two."

The biting of his neck, along with the scratching of his back urges him on. He pins her down and, taking some ice from a nearby glass, he lowers himself before her velvet fortress, he places the ice cube deep within her and she groans long and hard. He conquers her spur, licking and devouring all that she has to offer. Her legs start to tremble and her waist rolls back and forth. As her lower back stiffens, her body goes rigid as she cascades into his awaiting mouth. Her breathing pulses as she holds him there, trying to regain her senses. He kisses her body and finds a scar that he treats with the utmost attention, kissing it and biting at it. He flips her over and again breaks into her boundaries, pounding hard and fast as his muscles flex and stretch with his relentlessness. Leaning over, he kisses her back as he's throbbing inside her.

She turns, pushes him to the floor and claws at his legs and at the sign on his leg. She grabs him and lowers herself with all that she is, rolling her waist to and fro.

As he sucks and kisses her nipples and he feels her body rise, as again she reaches her peak and she falls to his chest, both their hearts pounding against one another.

His body lifts off the floor as he continues to thrust away, and as she feels him tighten, she escapes and takes him in her hands, releasing him over her body.

As his body expands and contracts in passion and desire, she stands and says, "Many men have tried and failed at what you've done. Most never last and yet, you, an unknown to the world, have conquered me."

The man stood as his shadow flew across the room and said, "I am quiet to the naked eye and have nothing to prove. Tell me, the scar you have, where did you get it?"

She said, "My heart was stolen long ago and that's the scar I carry."

She took her clothes and before she left she said, "The mark on your leg, what is it?"

The man smiled sinfully, "It's dark art, for the ink on my right thigh is that of a man changing into the Devil."

As I looked up, she had gone but my dark art still remains.

Exchanges

I often sit and wonder
If I'd trade The Dark Arts
And my Dark friend
To lead a plainer existence
It's not all smiles and laughter
And I would chance a thought at
Letting my gifts
Slip from grasp to see what
The numbness of nothing feels like
To be just another face
In the crowd
That passes many unkept buildings
And only to find
That in a void of silence
I'd find too many voices
I often wonder that
And I wonder if you do too.

Reflections

I know of a young man, who stood at the waters edge, peering
into it like a mirror. With him was a young boy, he too looked
on from the waters edge. The boy looked lost and hurt. The
young man said, "Why are you here, all alone?"

The young boy replied, "I am not alone."

The young man said, "Who else is here with you?"

The boy said, "My nightmares are here, but they are real and taunt
me."

The young man asked, "Why? You are just a child and should not
know of evil and wickedness."

The boy began to shake, "My life has been tainted by those I trust
and should love."

The young man replied, "Tell me of your hurt and I will try to
save you and heal you."

"You cannot save nor heal me," said the boy, "I have been beaten,
spat on and had my innocence stolen from me and it's lost
forever. I called for help but no one came, I cried until my
heart emptied and nobody dried my tears. I wanted a hug but
nobody wanted me."

The young man fell to his knees and broke in two. He looked up
to the sky and cried, and his sorrow was felt in the wind. He
said, "Please let me save you; I will wade into the darkness and
light up your world and nobody will ever harm you again."

The boy's eyes looked on and he smiled as though his innocence
had returned. "Would you do that? Would you save me with a
tear and love me with a smile?"

The young man said, "Oh yes I will, Please let's leave here."

The boy said, "You can free me, you don't have to wipe the tears from my eyes. You must wipe your own first and know in your heart that it's not your fault. You have saved me."

The young man wiped his tears and hope entered his world once more for the boy.

The boy said, "Sometimes bad things happen to good people, but even darkness can't last forever. There is always a ray of light, a ripple in the water that echoes out across a lake to reach the other side."

The young man said, "How do I save you? Show me, I can't bear it any more!"

The boy said, "Remember me always."

"I will," he replied.

"Pick up a pebble and cast it into the water."

He picked up the pebble and looked at the boy, who whispered "No fear, no crying, just gentleness."

The young man cast the pebble into the water and as ripples played out across the surface, the boy slowly vanished.

The man stood looking on and the water became calm. The boy changed.

The boy was the young man looking into the water, but the young man was not a stranger. He was a reflection of somebody I knew long ago, yes indeed, it was me.

Homeward Bound

I have walked many miles
Just to
Reach my home,
I have worn my feet out, right down
To the bloody bone,
These knees
Have bent more times than
Rock and stone
I carry all the burdens
That the gods fail to see,
But I know that
These demons won't ever let me be,
I'll carry the weights and chains
Pick the locks
And set you free
I have walked many miles
Just to reach my home,
And as I step through
The door
At last I'm not alone

Beyond Vision

I met an old, all-seeing man one day. I asked him, "Tell me kind sir, do you know of beauty, and where it can be found? For I wish to find it, many men I have seen have ladies that are like dreams to me."

The old man stared out into the void where a lake shimmered not far from us.

He said, "I will tell you what I know, and how I came to know of true beauty."

So we sat and the storyteller began his tale.

"Long ago, as the sun raised its weary head from the night's pillow which it had slept upon, there was a lady on the far side of the lake, who could often be seen swimming naked in the silvery, calm waters. Her skin was pale but flawless, with curves that few had seen. Yet many never wanted to, for she was said to be plainer than the desert in appearance and bore a small scar down her face. No man ever paid her a second glance.

She lived alone, had no family and very few, if any, visitors. She was unlike those that lived on the other side of the lake, preferring to keep to herself, watching the women who had such gifts she felt she did not own or would ever have."

"Tell me old man is there not someone for everyone out there?" I said.

He looked at me and said, "You have a great view of the world, I can tell, you see inner beauty, and that is rare insight indeed."

The old man continued to peer far into the distance. "Many claim to have seen, some have said they have even touched it but many haven't."

I asked him to continue the story, and so he did.

"She only ever crossed the lake to buy food and clothing as and when she needed it, but only at sunset when few would be able to see her. Little did they know she longed for a lover just like any other woman does. Those that did see her called her names and pointed at her, but what's worse was when they sometimes ignored her. For being shouted at meant that at least they did see her. She left before the cruel words became too much. As she did, she ran into a young man and his dog, that were in her path and he was knocked to the ground."

"Oh so sorry dear sir; I did not see you there, I am sorry."

The young man got up and said, "That's ok, for I did not see you either and my dog appears to be fine."

As the dog barked, in a kind gesture he reached out to her shoulder and touched her face. She smiled, and he said "What an amazing smile you have, it must be so stunning to see, but to touch is just as breathtaking as any adventure I have been on or heard of."

She looked at him intensely, and felt for a moment like many other women might have done in such moments as these. "You don't shy away from me, how so?" she said gently.

"I do not see like others, there is more to another than just using one's eyes. There is also the sense of touch, smell and warmness in a voice, if you permit me to listen to yours."

This was unlike her, for she never felt drawn to anyone and yet she couldn't disguise her smile when she was facing him. They sat and talked 'til the moon was at its highest in the sky, until the lake lay still and the town fell asleep.

"Tell me what you see when you look at me?" he said as his dog lay on his lap.

"I see you, that's what I see. I view you like anyone else and treat you no differently," she said.

The young mans eyes sparkled.

"And what of me?" she said, "You don't seem ill to look at me?"

"Why should I? All my life people have told me what is beautiful, what's acceptable.

I grow tired of their words, so I follow my heart and that's how I know you are too lovely for any one man to hold for too long."

Looking at the old man I could see he was reliving every word. Every breath he took sought love and emotion on the wind that blew through our hair.

"Tell me sir, what happened? Don't leave me guessing,.." I said.

The old man drew a long, deep breath and as I looked, a lonesome tear slipped down his aged face and vanished into his beard.

"Young sir there is nothing more to say. We met, we fell in love but in the end I let her go and that is why I weep, but it's tears of joy not sorrow."

"I don't understand?" I said.

He turns and asks me to stand up with him. Placing his hand on my shoulder, we begin to walk.

"There will come a time," he said, "When using your eyes is not enough, you need to close them. Make yourself deaf to what others tell you and then you will find real beauty."

He stops and I turn to face him, "Look at my pale blue eyes, you'd say they're lovely but I will have to take your word for it. I have never seen them for I am blind and she was so fair and amazing that I had to let her go."

We walked on until I saw the sunset and he felt it.

I don't understand what beauty is
And I guess I never will But I do know in order to see it
You also have to feel it,
Beauty is more than just skin deep.

Roses on the wind

"It was the way she smiled at me," said my friend from a distant
shore who had seen many places, and spent time in the
company of many ill-fated men and fools.

He said, "It's that moment like no other, when you are filled with
words that long to escape your lips, and yet they fail you
because your emotions are frozen by such an enchanting
sight."

I sat stolen by his lyrics, wanting to speak as he did, with no fear of
showing the world how I felt.

"Please continue," I said.

He did, and I struggle now to compose words that do his telling
justice.

He gazed lightly out onto the horizon, beyond the clouds and
further, "When she smiled, the mountains from up on high,
their peaks would melt and waves of snow came hurtling
down, yet no destruction was made. Her hair was long and
broke like waves over her shoulders, and when the wind blew,
it made the sound of leaves rustling on the ground in the
autumn."

He smiled and shook his head, and I could see that my friend
had seen an angel. He grew silent as his fingertips ran down
his face. The hairs on the back of my neck stood on end as I
watched and listened as he bared his soul before me.

"I only saw her the one time but that's all I needed, that's all
anyone should ever need.

Not countless encounters to see where paths lead, but an instant
connection, a storm if you will, of the heart that splits rocks,

parts oceans and burns like a dying star about to ignite the universe."

There and then I broke down and wept like a child lost in a vast space, all alone, at his amazing verse. He took from his pocket an old cloth, not like the shabby threads he wore, but a pure white cloth with a rose in each corner, and he dried my tears.

"It's ok son, you may not speak with words that can silence a great hall, but you yield foundations of the soul that few men dare to unveil to another being, and that in itself is priceless."

I looked at him and asked, "What of the woman you saw, did you speak to her? What did she say?"

He replied, "I did muster some words, but as she walked over to me a man tried to touch her in a way that is sinful if she is not your love. I fought the man and we struggled. In the rage and chaos of two Titans doing battle he pulled a gun and so did I, shots rang out and when the smoke cleared, there before the waking dawn lay the woman I spoke of."

Looking at my friend I could see the guilt had rotted him to his very core.

"What happened?" I begged him.

"In the confusion he grabbed the woman, the coward used her as a shield but my bullets had torn into her. He fled and I dropped to my knees and held her and cried. They were the last tears I'll ever shed in this life. She spoke to me as she lay slipping away."

"It's not your fault, I was coming to speak to you, to say hello but it seems instead it's goodbye."

"And she dried my tears with this cloth. She died there and then in my arms. I fled the scene and now we sit here, with you trying to convince me to come down."

My friend was right, for we sat high on a cliff top watching the clouds change shape,

and the sky tells its story with many colours.

"Tell me friend, you've brought me here to tell me about your life, to confess your guilt have you not?"

We both stood, and he hugged me tightly, an embrace that I can still feel today when I am lonely.

As I turned and took a few steps, a gust of wind passed through me. I looked round and he had gone, he leapt from the edge with no sound, no goodbyes but a warm hug that said it all, into the mountains below.

As the hurt started to build deep within me, a gust of wind blew up from the abyss below, and in it's clutches a white cloth with four roses on it. I snatched the cloth from the wind and wiped my eyes.

I lost my friend that day, and it breaks my heart to speak of such moments that will stay with me 'til I fade away. Yet I thank him, for without him I would not be able to tell the story the way I do.

I still have the cloth from that fateful day. I've lost a great friend and the gift of tears, but gained the power of words to tell our tale.

For without them we are all but speechless and hollow.

Feathers

I have followed my heart
And kept my word,
You kept me hidden and caged
Like a bird
I taught you to sing and showed you
How to dance,
But you made me hideous
So no one dared glance
I washed your body, kept you dry
And warm,
You saw to it I was broken
So desperate and torn
When I showed you love and gave
A warm embrace,
You beat me like an animal
And spat in my face
I have weathered the storm
And
The winds of time,
Watched you grow old and lose
Your mind
My feathers were so dull
Once scraggy and scythed,
But who would have thought
I could be saved
For time is a friend it works both ways,
It gives you life

But also slays
Now my feathers shine and you can't
Bear to see,
This bird you jailed longs to be free
So I will leave you now
To a life on your own,
You had your fun may you rot
To the bone
This is my life and my time has come,
To spread my wings
And fly into the sun.

Shades Of Skin

I had a girl a long time ago
She wouldn't stay the course
She melted like snow
I took time to listen
To her wants and needs,
But when I spoke
She never listened to me
I used my hands
To soothe her pain,
But she always left me
Out in the rain
I kissed her lips
And looked into her eyes,
But nothing was there,
Not even a disguise
Out in full view
For others to see,
You shunned my hand
So others wouldn't see
When we held hands
I'd squeeze you so tight,
But why should it matter
If I'm not white
I sat in the bath
With lights dimmed right down,
Doing my best to remove
This colour brown

I scrubbed so hard
To remove my skin,
Because I was told to mix with others
Is a great sin
I used many matches
To remove the stains,
But it was no use
It just left me in pain
I've been beaten, robbed
And knocked to the ground,
You never helped, never cried
You didn't even frown
It's not my fault
I am so out of place,
And I never knew
You were ashamed of my race
But that explains a lot
When you hid me out of sight,
The shades of my body
Can't be seen at night
All your friends just stood and laughed,
While your family screamed, held their mouths and
    gasped
Now I sit here
In this dark empty space,
Looking at a broken mirror
Trying to hide my face
But that's ok you got the problem
It was you, not me
I'll sit forever until another loves me

In The Park Without You

Ever been walking and seen
Others holding hands,
And wishing it was you?
And making life's little plans
Seeing them kiss, smile and stare,
I wish I had women so stunning and fair.
I often see them out in the park,
But no one sees me because I walk in the dark
I long for something more than
This empty feeling,
A touch of your skin is all
That I'm needing
And as I walk with my head low
To the ground
My heart beats so softly, so broken
And no sound
With my hands in my pockets
And no photos of you,
What else is left? If only dreams would come true
I will always be like this; I will always be alone,
This my story, it's already set in stone
As you can tell
It's plain to see that such
Amazing things never happen to me
So I will stand from afar
And watch many lovers
And when I sleep tonight I am
By myself naked under the covers.

Neglection Of Innocence

In a room like we have all seen and may have been in, where a
window is broken, the curtains are stained yellow and brown
and the walls are bare, lays a boy tied by his ankles to a bed.
His skin was pale as a ghost as he had hardly been in the sunlight;
his body was gaunt and punished from neglect and an absence
of love. While the boy lies there with no hope to keep him
company, he talks to himself.
"Another day here again and nobody to talk to, Not even the
floorboards creak to speak to me. Why nobody cares, or knows
that I am here, I don't know."
How sad he must have felt knowing that beyond the walls lay a
world that might never know him. As he lay there and the
light echoed in from the broken window, he suddenly felt that
he was not alone, but could not see anybody else in the room.
"Who's there?" he asked, but no reply was given.
He strained his eyes in the dim light and caught a glimpse of
someone or something watching him.
"Who's there, how did you get in here and is there a way out?"
Still no word was spoken. He struggles on the bed but the knots
are many years old and too tight to undo.
"You can't leave this room, not like this anyway." said a quiet
voice.
The boy now in shock, screams that high pitched scream that
turns your blood cold.
"Help me, can you not untie me???"
"I could." said the voice, "But what's the use? You can't leave here
because you don't want to."

The poor boy said, "I want to. I hate it here and long to be free, for this life does not want or love me."

The sun outside had now fallen and the night crept into the forgotten room. With very little light the voice came closer and the boy now felt the weight of him sitting on the bed. They talked for many hours, asking how they each came to be there.

The new friend said to the boy, "Do you really want to leave this room? Will you take me with you? As I don't want to stay anymore."

The boy sat up and said, "Of course I will, but why did you stay? Why didn't you go before?"

"Because I was afraid to be alone, if we go together, it's company for us both."

"Then let us go," replied the boy. "Untie these knots and we will flee this place."

But as he said this, the knots had already been untied.

The boy now free from the bed posts said, "How do we get out? For I believe the door is locked, it's too dark to see and the window is too high to reach."

"Just wait a moment." said the voice.

The boy cried, "We have to leave!"

"And you will, I promise you."

The dawn broke outside and burst into the room like never before, the light hit the floorboards and clasped at the door handle.

"Let's go." shouted the now newly free boy, and he grabbed the boy's hand and ran to the door. To his amazement the door handle turned with ease and opened. The forgotten boy stepped from the room into a dazzling sunrise. He turns and sees the other boy pointing at the bed. As he looks across he sees himself still lying there.

"I don't understand I thought I'd escaped???"

"And you have," said the other boy whose face came into view,

"Look and see"

As he looked on, he saw the boy on the bed vanish and the reflection of his spirit fade

And then it dawns on him. Nobody knew he was there, he had been forgotten, and floorboards don't speak to the living, or to those that have passed on but don't know it.

With that he closes the door behind him, and walks off into a new sunrise, a place where darkness fails to enter.

How many children are locked up and forgotten?
How many are neglected and unloved?
I have a key and with it we'll set them free.

Footprints

Now the day has come,
And the time is here.
I know you'll still remember me
With a silent tear
When the days are sunny
And you're walking
In the park,
You'll feel me when
The wind blows
Singing in your hearts
If the nights are lonely
And you all feel cold,
Hold on to our memories
May they warm
You on your pillow
My bed I used to sleep in
Still carries
My body's scent,
You told me I was special
Dad, you said I was heaven-sent
There is an empty chair
Which I used to grace,
Recalling all the laughter
I've gone to that
Sunset place
Please don't be afraid
To feel so hurt and sad,

Those moments in my life
Are the best I ever had
Mum we talked and laughed
We even danced
In the pouring rain,
These feelings of your loss
No heartfelt words can explain
But now the time
Has come
And I have to sadly go,
Where I venture now
You cannot surely follow
I'm carried on the wind
Like the autumn leaves,
You'll hear my voice whispering
Blowing through the trees
Thank you Mum and Dad
Tell my brother I love him so,
He'll find my spirit playing
By the footsteps
In the snow
I love you all so much
Until the very end,
May these gentle words
Comfort you
Until we meet again. .

In loving memory of
Abby Gail Mcghee
Who passed away at the tender age of 7 years old
On October 14th 2013.
Sorely missed
But forever remembered
By those who love her.

Noose

A stranger once said to me
"Tone, it's an amazing world and
A wonderful life
And what a shame it is, that in time
We will be lost forever
In a dark sea of sleep
And others won't get to meet us."
I looked at him and I had to agree
"Yes my dear sir, you are right
For all must bend and give way
To the decay of time."
And so he put his arm around me
Wiped the tear
That plummeted down my cheek and said
"You won't know this,
But we will miss you when you've gone
And talk of the many deeds you did."
And I thanked him for that's all I could do,
"For I will miss this life
But will always be remembered.".
And then he placed the noose around my neck
And my world
Went dark.

Afterword

I would like to
Thank you greatly for reading my book
It's a shame I can't do it in person
But sadly this is where I leave you
Looking at a page filled with just a few short lines and wondering
Is this it? What, there's no more?
And like I said
Sadly this is where I leave you ....
For now.

Acknowledgements

I would like to thank the following people for allowing me to verse for them, for without them these pages would be blank and empty.

Aric W. Hoogerwerf, Cathy Wooler, Christine Wooler, Carley Jackson, Catherine Suddaby, Emma Ellis, Michelle Collins, Tracey Sanders, Anouska Young, Rob Brook, Tricia Dean, Angel Louise, Loria Warren.

I would also like to thank Shaun and Mhairi Goodwin for all your painstaking hours of reading and printing and driving you mad. No doubt I'll get hit with your frying pan if I ever decide to do another book.

Many thanks to Simon Jenkins for all his hard work with the front cover and how you captured the title of my book so gracefully.

I would also like to thank my close and personal friend Ivor Larby, for if it had not been for you, it would have taken me two lifetimes to make this achievable.

Lightning Source UK Ltd.
Milton Keynes UK
UKOW05f0034310514

232635UK00005B/59/P